Neither Male Nor Female

by
Betty Miller

First Edition Published 1980
Second Printing 1982
Third Printing 1983
Fourth Printing 1984
Fifth Printing 1987
Sixth Printing 1988
Seventh Printing 1989
Eighth Printing 1994
Ninth Printing 2001
Tenth Printing 2003

Neither Male Nor Female

ISBN 1-57149-012-4

CHRIST UNLIMITED MINISTRIES, INC.
Pastor R.S. (Bud) Miller - Publisher
P.O. Box 850
Dewey, Arizona 86327
All Rights Reserved

Printed in U.S.A.

Scripture quotations are taken from the King James Version
unless otherwise indicated.

Contents

Preface

Greetings in the name of our Lord Jesus Christ:

I present this book to the body of Christ as the Holy Spirit presented it to me. I challenge you to allow God's Spirit of truth, and the Bible, to test the accuracy of the words within these pages. This book, part of the Overcoming Life Series, is also addressed to all seekers of truth who know not THE CHRIST UNLIMITED, as it would be my privilege to introduce you to Him.

During the early years of the ministry, I struggled to learn how to hear the voice of God. Once, while nervously waiting to speak before a large audience, and not being sure on what subject I should speak, I posed to the Lord in prayer this question: "Lord, what am I going to say to all these people?" In my spirit, I heard Him very clearly reply, "Betty, I was hoping you would not say anything, as I really wanted to speak." Yes, He wants to speak through us, as we yield to His Spirit. Submitting to the Lord and the guidance of the Holy Spirit, I found, was not only possible, but the only way He wants us to minister. **For it is not ye that speak, but the Spirit of your Father which speaketh in you (Matthew 10:20).**

This book is a gift from the Holy Spirit. I take no credit for it. If something within these pages blesses you, enlightens you, brings you closer to the Lord, releases you from fear or bondage, or heals or delivers you, then please lift your voice in praise to the precious Savior of our souls, Jesus Christ our Lord! On the other hand, if you find some of these things difficult to receive, hard to understand, or totally heretical from your viewpoint, would you also look to the Lord and ask Him if it could possibly be the truth? With an open and honest heart, will you ask God to change any pre-conceived ideas, and be free from traditions to receive of Him, His truth? His truth always brings freedom, never bondage. **And ye shall know the truth, and the truth shall make you free (John 8:32).**

In walking with the Lord, I have found we must obey the

v

things we feel He is speaking to us. In my personal life, I used to be fearful of speaking for the Lord because I was so afraid of missing Him and making mistakes. (He, of course, has now delivered me of all my fears. Praise Him!) He encouraged me not to quit because of mistakes when He spoke these words to me: "Betty, if I receive the glory and praise for all the things that are a blessing to people, I also receive the responsibility for your mistakes, as long as you are striving to please me. I am able to make even those work for your good." **And we know that all things work together for good to them that love God, to them who are the called according to his purpose (Romans 8:28).** We serve a wonderful, loving God, who encourages us to follow and obey Him that we might be blessed, and in turn bless others!

This book was written as an act of obedience to the Lord, whom I dearly love. I consider it an honor to write for Him. Years ago, when I was in prayer, the Lord spoke that I was to write a book, but I never felt it was God's timing, nor did I feel the unction or anointing to begin this work until now. Over the past year God has performed a series of miracles to confirm that it is now His time, and has made the arrangements for this to become a reality.

I pray that this book, along with the Overcoming Life Series, may help you learn to walk closer to our Lord, as He is THE CHRIST UNLIMITED!

I am, by His love,
A handmaiden of the Lord,

Betty Miller
February, 1980

If any man will do his will, he shall know of the doctrine, whether it be of God, or whether I speak of myself (John 7:17).

Foreword

It just seemed natural that I would do the foreword on this book since my wife, Betty, and myself, are "one flesh." God, through the Holy Spirit, has given by revelation to Betty many truths of His Word, which have been set forth in this book.

The Lord spoke to Betty about ten years ago that she was to write a book for Him, and that He would arrange the right time and place to write it. Betty simply took this vision and set it aside until God began to "quicken" her spirit to bring it forth. One morning, very early, Betty awakened, and began to write as the Lord dictated to her. In giving her this small initial portion of the book, he showed her how, by submitting to His Spirit, and completely yielding to Him, He would feed to her the message He wanted to share with the body of Christ. He also revealed how quickly and easily it would be completed. The messages that God has given in this Overcoming Life Series are to all who desire to become "overcomers" and be "conformed to the image of His son" (**Romans 8:29**). Our Lord is not satisfied that a person remains a "babe" in Christ, but longs for each "babe" to grow to maturity. He desires that we should strive to become overcomers, live the overcoming life, and claim the promises of the inheritance of all things that are to be given to the overcomers.

I thank God that He has allowed me to share such close love and companionship with Betty. I know that within her heart she has no personal ambitions, no personal ends to achieve. Betty has simply been doing the will of the Father in the writing of this anointed book. May the Lord bless you with this book, as He has blessed us in being a part of His work.

Yours in Christ,

Pastor R.S. (Bud) Miller

He that overcometh shall inherit all things; and I will be his God and he shall be my son (Revelation 21:7).

Credits & Acknowledgments

ALL PRAISE AND CREDIT
GOES TO **THE CHRIST UNLIMITED!**

Truly Christ, the Father, and the Holy Spirit, are to be praised, not only for this book, but for our very lives. His sacrifice on Calvary made it possible to know Him and all the members of God's family.

As with the printing of any book, there are lots of people responsible for the words on these pages, physical words as well as spiritual words. All the people that have ever been a part of my life, all the people that have prayed and supported this ministry, my friends and my family have truly contributed to this work. Special credit should be given to my husband, Bud, whose faithful and loving prayers, encouragement, leadership, and love are a big part of this book. Also, to everyone whose books and articles I've read, to the ministers of the Gospel, whose sermons I've heard, I express my gratitude. For each has contributed, in some measure, to this book. The list is endless, but eternity has the records. So instead of naming individuals on this page and giving them earthly credit, I prefer the Lord Jesus Christ to reward them each as only He can. God bless you all, and may you be surprised as you open up the box that contains your heavenly treasures.

For the Son of man shall come in the glory of his Father with his angels; and then he shall reward every man according to his works (Matthew 16:27).

Introduction

NEITHER MALE NOR FEMALE deals with many issues in regard to a woman's role in the church, plus many women related concerns.

Some of the issues discussed are "Who is a woman's spiritual head and covering?" and "Does God call women to the five-fold ministry?" Also find out what God's Word says about divorce, celibacy, choosing a marriage partner, and other women related topics.

The feminist movement in the world that is asserting women's rights is not the way God liberates His women. Many of these are angry and demanding! When the Holy Spirit calls a woman to ministry, they become submissive handmaidens of the Lord. *NEITHER MALE NOR FEMALE* gives scriptural references and examples of many women that God used in the Bible.

This book also helps women to have the proper relationship with their husbands and children. Only God can truly liberate His women to serve Him and become all that He desires them to be as wives and mothers.

Neither Male
Nor Female

Galatians 3:28: There is neither Jew nor Greek, there is neither bond nor free, there is neither male nor female: for ye are all one in Christ Jesus.

Women's True Liberation

One subject that has caused much controversy among many Christians is the discussion of what place a woman has in the church. As with every other question that is controversial, we should look to the Word of God for our answers and be willing to set aside our traditional teachings and preconceived ideas. God's Word is always the final authority on every subject.

What does God's Word say about women ministering, teaching and submitting to males? In this hour, Women's Liberation has discolored the true picture of a woman's rightful place in the kingdom of God. Women's Liberation has degraded womanhood and destroyed the respect a woman should have in her elevated position. The Lord has lifted fallen woman and given her not only a beautiful role in family life, but also set before her the privilege of entering into the overcoming life with Him. Because of the world's false standards, she now has become a competitive, covetous and vain creature. The Lord has such a lofty plan, not only for all women, but also for all who will follow Him.

Women's Liberation has brought greater burdens upon women rather than liberating them as they support so many things that are sinful in the eyes of God. Abortion is a terrible sin of murder; yet millions of women have committed this crime, many without realizing the terrible curse, guilt and emotional sickness that comes with it. The Women's Lib Movement supports not only abortion, but also other so-called freedoms of choice and equal rights that are abominations to God. The only way for any woman to be free is to give her life to the Lord Jesus Christ and to walk in His freedom and liberation. There have been great women of the Bible whose lives still inspire us today to stand and be counted with them as women of God. Women's Lib is the counterfeit to what God has for those women who would follow him.

Male and Female Created He Them

Jesus did a beautiful thing for women through His sacrifice on Calvary. He redeemed them from the curse of the law and liberated them to the original position He had planned for them. All of mankind was under a curse because of the disobedience of the first man and woman; however, God made a way through another man, Jesus Christ, to redeem man from the curse.

When the Bible speaks of man, the general reference is to both male and female, as they both constitute "mankind." **So God created man in his own image, in the image of God created he him; male and female created he them (Genesis 1:27). Male and female created he them; and blessed them, and called their name Adam, in the day when they were created (Genesis 5:2).** God had not intended for man to fall under the curse; however, due to his disobedience sin resulted, and the penalty for sin was the curse. God, in His mercy, still loved mankind and provided a way for him to rise from his fall and be restored to his true destiny. **For since by man came death, by man came also the resurrection of the dead. For as in Adam all die, even so in Christ shall all be made alive (I Corinthians 15:21-22). And so it is written, The first man Adam was made a living soul; the last Adam was made a quickening spirit. Howbeit that was not first which is spiritual, but that which is natural; and afterward that which is spiritual. The first man is of the earth,**

2

earthy: the second man is the Lord from heaven. As is the earthy, such are they also that are earthy; and as is the heavenly, such are they also that are heavenly. And as we have borne the image of the earthy, we shall also bear the image of the heavenly. Now this I say, brethren, that flesh and blood cannot inherit the kingdom of God; neither doth corruption inherit incorruption (I Corinthians 15:45-50).

The first revelation we need to receive regarding women is that they are all cursed (along with men) and cannot rise above that curse until they receive Jesus in their hearts. "Flesh and blood cannot inherit the kingdom of God," and the only way a man or woman can "bear the image of the heavenly" is to be "born again." Once we are born into the kingdom of God, we become new creatures in Christ. In the Spirit then, we find there is "neither male nor female," just as there are no race distinctions nor class separations. The Lord looks on the hearts of His new creatures and therefore does not discriminate when He offers His love and privileges. Women are not excluded from any of God's promises nor callings because of their sex.

Women as Ministers

Tradition has attempted to exclude them from certain ministries; however, God's Word does not. Those that are dogmatic in excluding women from the ministries of God usually are not walking in the Spirit, as they see women after the flesh (viewing her sex), not after the Spirit (seeing her heart and calling). The Lord admonishes us in His Word that we are not to look at one another with regard to our sex, race, class or culture, but rather we are to see one another through spiritual eyes.

Wherefore henceforth know we no man after the flesh: yea, though we have known Christ after the flesh, yet now henceforth know we him no more. Therefore if any man be in Christ, he is a new creature: old things are passed away; behold, all things are become new. And all things are of God, who hath reconciled us to himself by Jesus Christ, and hath given to us the ministry of reconciliation: To wit, that God was in Christ, reconciling the world unto himself, not imputing their trespasses unto them; and hath committed unto us the word of reconciliation. Now then we are ambassadors for Christ, as though God did beseech you by us: we pray you in Christ's stead, be ye reconciled to God (II Corinthians 5:16-20).

God wants to use any person who will yield to His Spirit, regardless of that person's sex or capabilities, as the new creature has His capabilities. The word "man" in the above verses in the original Greek does not mean the male sex, but rather all of mankind. Therefore, He has called not only men to minister the word of reconciliation, but also women. Ambassadors are those who are sent on a mission representing whoever sends them. If we are sent by Christ, then we are His representatives.

Many of the difficulties that are encountered with women ministering are because some of them have not been sent, but rather have set out on their own. However, if they are sent by God, He will empower them and equip them for the task for which He calls them. The same is true with men who attempt to minister without the Lord's sending and equipping. Many traditional teachings have forbidden women from teaching because of two isolated verses in the Word of God (I Corinthians 14:34 and I Timothy 2:11,12), ignoring the many others that teach otherwise. (We will discuss these later.) It has always been a strange doctrine that will allow women to go to foreign mission fields and teach heathen men, but will not allow the "heathen" men here in America to be taught by the same women. This stems from failing to understand the whole counsel of God in regard to a woman's position in the church. It makes absolutely no sense to think that a female who is learned in the Scriptures cannot teach a male who is unlearned.

Our problem is that we must see there are rules for the fleshly,

4

or earthly man, and there are rules for the spiritual man. Then, we must discern when to apply the appropriate Scripture. We are admonished in **II Timothy 2:15** to **Study to show thyself approved unto God, a workman that needeth not to be ashamed, rightly dividing the word of truth.** In the Spirit, women are equal with men, and each must submit unto Jesus as the spiritual head. In the flesh, in the marriage relationship, women are to be subject to their husband's headship. The Lord ordained that the man be the one that would make final decisions in the home because in any relationship involving two people one must be the final authority. In the marriage, or fleshly relationship, the man is the head and should guide his home and family. In the spirit, Jesus Christ is the head of His family and He guides each member according to His headship. **Submitting yourselves one to another in the fear of God. Wives, submit yourselves unto your own husbands, as unto the Lord. For the husband is the head of the wife, even as Christ is the head of the church: and He is the saviour of the body. Therefore as the church is subject unto Christ, so let the wives be to their own husbands in everything. Husbands, love your wives, even as Christ also loved the church, and gave himself for it; That he might sanctify and cleanse it with the washing of water by the word, That he might present it to himself a glorious church, not having spot, or wrinkle, or any such thing; but that it should be holy and without blemish. So ought men to love their wives as their own bodies. He that loveth his wife loveth himself. For no man ever yet hated his own flesh; but nourisheth and cherisheth it, even as the Lord the church: For we are members of his body, of his flesh, and of his bones. For this cause shall a man leave his father and mother, and shall be joined unto his wife, and they two shall be one flesh. This is a great mystery: but I speak concerning Christ and the church. Nevertheless let every one of you in particular so love his wife even as himself; and the wife see that she reverence her husband (Ephesians 5:21-33).**

Submission to a husband does not mean a woman is to be a slave in bondage to that man, but rather it is to be a mutual submission in love. Verse 21 of the above Scripture says we are to submit unto each other. Submission means to yield or "to set yourself under." From this definition we see we are to yield to one another instead of demanding our own way.

Love should be the rule in our homes, and we should "prefer one another." Not only should this be especially true in our homes, but in our church family as well. **Be kindly affectioned one to another with brotherly love; in honour preferring one another (Romans 12:10)**. Both husband and wife should be submissive and loving. The love of Christ should be the rule in the home. When wifely submission is over stressed we find it can lead to many problems that cause the husband-wife relationship to be thrown out of balance. Some even stress it to the degree that a wife must obey every command her husband dictates to her. They arrive at this conclusion because of the Scripture, **Therefore as the church is subject unto Christ, so let the wives be to their own husbands in everything (Ephesians 5:24).** The word "everything" here is not inclusive of evil things. Women are to submit to their husbands as the church is to submit unto Christ. Christ would never ask anything of the church that was not according to God's Word. Women are never to submit unto things that do not line up with God's Word.

A perfect example of this is the New Testament account of Ananias and Sapphira. Chapter 5 of Acts records the story of how this couple conspired to hold back what they had agreed to give unto the church. The church had not asked them for anything; it was their own decision to contribute the money from the sale of their land. When the land sold, they conspired to keep back a portion of the money. However, when Ananias gave the money to the apostles, he lied and told them it was the full amount. The Holy Spirit revealed this evil lie to Peter and showed him that Satan had entered Ananias' heart. Because he lied to God, he instantly fell dead at the apostle's feet. Sapphira, Ananias' wife, later came along and upon telling the same lie, also fell dead. If she had not submitted to her husband and agreed to this evil, her life would have been spared. However, she followed in her husband's evil; thus she suffered the same fate. This should show us clearly that to submit to the evil in a husband's life will only bring destruction upon the woman.

True Submission

There are Scriptures that give us a guideline as to how far any human being is to submit to another. Our first submission should be unto the Lord. **Jesus said unto him, Thou shalt love the Lord thy God with all thy heart, and with all thy soul, and with all thy mind (Matthew 22:37).** If any man, husband or otherwise, would ask us to do something that Jesus would not sanction, then we must refuse to do it. We should also do and apply those things the Holy Spirit would speak to us. We must obey Him over what man would say to us. If it is truly the Lord speaking to us, He will deal with the husband who is wrong.

And they called them, and commanded them not to speak at all nor teach in the name of Jesus. But Peter and John answered and said unto them, Whether it be right in the sight of God to hearken unto you more than unto God, judge ye. For we cannot but speak the things which we have seen and heard (Acts 4:18-20).

If we are submitted unto the Lord and our husband is requiring things of us that we feel are not of the Lord, we should take the matter to the Lord and ask for His wisdom on how to deal with it. We should pray for our husbands and ask the Lord to speak to them if they are in the wrong. However, we should also be willing to be corrected if we are in the wrong. We should ask the Holy Spirit to resolve the conflict and to deal with the party who is wrong, and both should be willing to change an opinion.

The Holy Spirit generally will not ask a woman to do something that would cause her to disobey her husband and thereby cause conflict in her home. Most women who have a problem submitting to their husbands have the same problem submitting to the Lord. Our relationship with the Lord will reflect in our attitudes with not only our husbands and children, but with all others as well. If we please the Lord and obey Him, we will find we will have favor with the people in our lives. And, to those who do not understand us and spitefully use us, we shall have God's grace to bear their persecution and God's love toward them to forgive them.

There are several accounts in the Word of God that plainly teach submission to God over submission to husbands. One familiar story is that of Mary, the mother of Christ (**Luke 1:26-38; Matthew 1:18-25**). She yielded to what God asked her to do without asking Joseph what he thought about it. In fact, he wanted to put her away when he found out she was pregnant. Surely Mary tried to explain to Joseph that this child was conceived by the Holy Ghost, but he could not receive her explanation until the Lord sent an angel to confirm to him that she indeed had heard the Lord. This is a case where a woman submitted to God first, and then the Lord dealt with her husband showing him she had heard the Lord.

All through the Bible we find accounts of God speaking to women before speaking to their husbands. Peter speaks of Sarah as a model wife in that he says in **I Peter 3:5-6, For after this manner in the old time the holy women also, who trusted in God, adorned themselves, being in subjection unto their own husbands: Even as Sarah obeyed Abraham, calling him lord: whose daughters ye are, as long as ye do well, and are not afraid with any amazement.**

Genesis 16:5-6 gives us another side of the picture, for we have here an account of a disagreement between Sarah and Abraham. On this occasion, Abraham conceded and allowed Sarah to have her way. We notice that God justified her for this in **Genesis 21:10-12** when the question came up again. God told Abraham to obey Sarah: **...Cast out this bondwoman and her**

8

**son: for the son of this bondwoman shall not be heir with my
son, even with Isaac. And the thing was very grievous in
Abraham's sight because of his son. And God said unto
Abraham, Let it not be grievous in thy sight because of the
lad, and because of thy bondwoman; in all that Sarah hath
said unto thee, hearken unto her voice; for in Isaac shall thy
seed be called.**

When the Scripture speaks of wives obeying and submitting
to their husbands, it cannot mean that every wife must obey her
husband always in everything. She, as well as he, is responsible to
obey what the Spirit gives each to do. The husband does not lead
the wife into all truth since this is the work of the Holy Spirit. This
does not license a wife who has a domineering spirit to do anything she wants simply because she says she is only subject to the
Lord. The Lord is displeased with any person who tries to domi-
nate and rule another's life, whether that person be male or female. There is nothing worse than a domineering, nagging wife.
Proverbs 21:9 expresses it this way, **It is better to dwell in a
corner of the housetop, than with a brawling woman in a
wide house.** Some women preachers have become very over-
bearing and bossy; thus it is very distasteful to hear them preach.
It is not necessarily what they are preaching that is wrong, but
their domineering and dictating spirits are wrong. This kind of
spirit is not of the Lord, whether it be in a man or woman.

The main thing for women to do in regard to following and
obeying what they feel the Lord is telling them to do is to be sure
it is the Lord. If it is the Lord, He will justify them as He did Sarah
and other women of the Bible. If it is not the Lord, they will create for themselves a lot of problems, not only with their husbands,
but with others as well.

Women who are single are not under any earthly man's
headship since they do not have a flesh relationship with a man.
Their head is Jesus Christ and it is this union to which they are
subject. **Wherefore, my brethren, ye also are become dead to
the law by the body of Christ; that ye should be married to**

9

another, even to him who is raised from the dead, that we should bring forth fruit unto God" (Romans 7:4).

Most Christian women experience two marriages. They are married to Christ and they are married to their husbands. The first is a spiritual marriage, the other an earthly or fleshly marriage. They are to be obedient to both. If they obey their spiritual head, they will not be disobeying their physical head, even if it is against what their husbands command because God will deal with their husbands. Some women are unequally yoked and have difficulty submitting to the desires of their ungodly husbands. They are to obey them as long as it does not mean disobedience to Christ. They are not to obey them if it would be morally or spiritually wrong.

A Biblical account of this can be found in **I Samuel 25:4-42**. Abigail was a woman who knew God. She was the wife of Nabal, an ungodly husband. She realized her husband's refusal to give gifts unto David's men endangered her whole household. On her own initiative she took food and rode to meet David. She was a wise woman; by disobeying her husband, she saved his life; for David would have slain him. She saved not only her husband's life, but also her own and her household's lives and possessions. She also found favor with David and with God. Her wicked husband Nabal died shortly after this as his heart was cold toward God. He was a son of Belial (another name for Satan).

Now therefore know and consider what thou wilt do; for evil is determined against our master, and against all his household: for he is such a son of Belial, that a man cannot speak to him. Then Abigail made haste, and took two hundred loaves, and two bottles of wine, and five sheep ready dressed, and five measures of parched corn, and an hundred clusters of raisins, and two hundred cakes of figs, and laid them on asses. And she said unto her servants, Go on before me; behold, I come after you. But she told not her husband Nabal...So David received of her hand that which she had brought him, and said unto her, Go up in peace to thine house; see, I have hear-

10

kened to thy voice, and have accepted thy person. **And Abigail came to Nabal; and behold, he held a feast in his house, like the feast of a king; and Nabal's heart was merry within him, for he was very drunken: wherefore she told him nothing, less or more, until the morning light. But it came to pass in the morning, when the wine was gone out of Nabal, and his wife had told him these things, that his heart died within him, and be became as a stone (I Samuel 25:17-19 and 35-37).**

Another account of a woman who moved in faith and was responsible for the salvation of her whole household was the harlot Rahab in chapters 2 and 6 of Joshua. There were men in her household but none of them had the faith and boldness to seek deliverance. **And Joshua saved Rahab the harlot alive, and her father's household, and all that she had; and she dwelleth in Israel even unto this day; because she hid the messengers, which Joshua sent to spy out Jericho (Joshua 6:25).**

Women today who move in faith and obedience to God can be responsible for the salvation of their households. Prayer can bring whole families to the Lord, even if at first the family members object to spiritual things. Later, they will be eternally grateful that someone stood and believed for their souls. It would be quite a revelation to take an inventory of how many men came to know the Lord Jesus as a result of the faith of some woman. We've heard thousands of testimonies of men who were saved as the direct result of a praying mother, wife or girlfriend. The first woman, Eve, may have led her man astray, but since then God has used many women to bring men back to Him. What a privilege to believe for our entire families. Allegiance and submission to the Lord bring miracles of deliverance.

Submission Out of Balance

Submission has been out of balance in both directions, thereby causing much confusion in the body of Christ. Those who refuse to submit to any authority are just as out of balance as those who submit to every dictate of those who they feel are their superiors, regardless of the mandates. We must have the leadership of the Holy Spirit in all areas of our lives. Legalistic approaches to the Word of God always bring bondage. Paul's letter to the Galatians was a reprimand to the people who were leaving the simplicity of the gospel and reverting back to strict rules and regulations.

We have the same problem today within the church as some are becoming hard and dogmatic in dealing with the truth and with people. Submission is required of God's people, but never to the point that men begin ruling other men's or women's lives. This has been abused greatly in regard to church authority. Some pastors have become dictators, while others have become so permissive (all in the name of love) that order is lost in the church. With no order in the body of Christ there is chaos. There has to be respect for the pastor and the other offices in the body of Christ. Any legalistic approach to this, however, brings bondage and does not carry out God's wishes. God's true pastors lead His flock in love and by example. **Neither as being lords over God's heritage, but being ensamples to the flock (I Peter 5:3).** These kind of church leaders and pastors are the ones the Lord has chosen to guide His people.

If you are in an area where this kind of ministry does not exist, you can pray for the Lord to send someone who will have a heart like His heart. In the meantime, He can furnish you with good books and taped teachings that can bring life to your spirit. He can bring the five-fold ministry to you as you sit under these teachings and learn through them. We are blessed in the hour we live to have the availability of books written by ministers throughout the ages. We can learn much through their writings. Of course, our greatest teaching tool is the Word of God, and the greatest teacher is the Holy Spirit.

God's plan is for all of His people to be part of a local body. If your heart is truly crying for a good shepherd, the Lord will move you to one or raise up one where you are. It may be a small group, but size is not the issue with God; the issue is relationships and submission. **Matthew 18:20** says, **For where two or three are gathered together in my name, there am I in the midst of them.**

Submission to True Elders

God's true ministers are the ones to which we are to submit as the Scripture says,

Obey them that have the rule over you, and submit your-selves: for they watch for your souls, as they that must give account... (Hebrews 13:17). Likewise, ye younger, submit yourselves unto the elder. Yea, all of you be subject one to another, and be clothed with humility: for God resisteth the proud, and giveth grace to the humble (I Peter 5:5).

The command here to submit unto the elder is not referring to what we generally term as elders in the church, but rather to those who are older and more knowledgeable in the Lord. Elder women are used of the Lord to help guide young Christians, male or female, as it certainly does not make sense for a young male convert to instruct a woman who has walked with the Lord for many years, simply because he is of male sex.

The Word of God demands respect for the elders, male and female. **Rebuke not an elder, but intreat him as a father; and the younger men as brethren; The elder women as mothers; the younger as sisters, with all purity (I Timothy 5:1-2).** God uses those vessels who have matured in Him to help others come to maturity.

The elders which are among you I exhort, who am also an elder, and a witness of the sufferings of Christ, and also a partaker of the glory that shall be revealed: Feed the flock of God which is among you, taking the oversight thereof, not by constraint, but willingly; not for filthy lucre, but of a ready mind (I Peter 5:1-2).

The Five-Fold Ministry

The Lord gave the church gifts of His choosing in the form of men and women who would lead the church into perfection (**Ephesians 4:8-12**).

It is the Lord who calls men and women to His ministry. He does not call special people, but the call goes out to "whosoever will." First, we are called to salvation; then as we walk in obedience to Him, He calls for us to be baptized in His Holy Spirit. As we continue to obey and follow Him, He then may choose us to serve Him in a full-time ministry. He chooses people for the ministry out of those who have walked in obedience to His other calls. He desires that all follow, but can only choose those who are obedient. These men and women who have answered the call are set in the ministry by Jesus Himself. Man's ordination does not qualify them, but the ordination of God does. Men will recognize those who are truly called by Him. They will even recognize women who are called of God as God empowers them with His anointing and power.

God has used many modern day women in His service as well as women spoken of in the Bible. Madame Guyon, Jessie Penn-Lewis, Aimee Semple McPherson and Kathryn Kuhlman are only a few of the women on the list of great five-fold ministry gifts to the church. What are those gifts and that ministry? **And His gifts were (varied; He Himself appointed and gave men to us,) some to be apostles (special messengers), some prophets (inspired preachers and expounders), some evangelists (preachers of the Gospel, traveling missionaries), some pastors (shepherds of His flock) and teachers (Ephesians 4:11 Amp.).**

When this Scripture says, "appointed and gave men to us," it does not mean just the male sex. The same man whom God created in the beginning which included male and female is the one referred to here. These "men" are both male and female and they have a responsibility to bring others into the maturity that they possess. **Ephesians 4** continues, **His intention was the perfecting and the full equipping of the saints (His consecrated people), [that they should do] the work of ministering toward building up Christ's body (the church), [That it might develop] until we all attain oneness in the faith and in the comprehension of the full and accurate knowledge of the Son of God; that [we might arrive] at really mature manhood....the completeness of personality which is nothing less than the standard height of Christ's own perfection -- the measure of the stature of the fullness of the Christ, and the completeness found in Him (Ephesians 4:12-13 Amp.).**

The Lord has lofty intentions for His men and women and desires that they come into perfection and maturity even as Christ walked in that perfection. The Lord sends those whom He chooses to bring about this maturing and perfecting. If we have been raised in a traditional church, the idea of coming into perfection will sound impossible and we will not be able to understand God's full intention for His body. The separation of laity and clergy is not God's plan for His people. All that are called to salvation are called to a full-time ministry in the Lord. This does not mean that all should leave their secular occupations, but all should devote their lives to the Lord and be as committed and active in witnessing, learning and growing in God as the leadership.

The leadership that God raises up is those men and women whom He trains for His work in the kingdom. We have been limited in our traditional churches to certain positions that men would give us, but the Lord is restoring His full five-fold ministry in these last days to prepare the body of Christ for His return.

Office of Apostle

The first ministry listed is that of apostle. When we hear this word, perhaps we think only of the original twelve apostles who walked with Jesus and the Apostle Paul. However, God has always had His apostles throughout the ages, and He has them in the earth today. The Greek meaning of the word apostle is "one sent forth." Anyone God sends forth to establish His kingdom and accomplish a special mission ordained of God is rightfully an apostle. These men and women of God do not have to tell others of their office because the body of Christ can recognize God's power and anointing upon them. It might sound strange to some to think that women can be apostles, but if they are sent forth by God, they qualify. Paul was not only called to be an apostle by God, but also was given a special miracle anointing distinguishing him as that ordained apostle of God. He had a special message and a special anointing.

Paul, a servant of Jesus Christ, called to be an apostle, separated unto the gospel of God (Romans 1:1). And God wrought special miracles by the hands of Paul (Acts 19:11).

Office of Prophet

The prophet is another office listed as part of this five-fold ministry. The woman who preaches and expounds God's Word and will is known as a prophetess. Prophets and prophetesses speak divine utterances at the unction of the Holy Spirit.

In the office of a prophet, one is given futuristic insights and knowledge of things to come. Prophets are used to identify the timing of prophetic events plus are given warning cries when impending judgment is near. God's Word predicted that in the last days He would use women in this office as well as men.

And it shall come to pass in the last days, saith God, I will pour out of my Spirit upon all flesh: and your sons and your daughters shall prophesy, and your young men shall see visions, and your old men shall dream dreams: And on my servants and on my handmaidens I will pour out in those days of my Spirit; and they shall prophesy (Acts 2:17-18).

16

God is pouring out His Spirit upon all flesh, male and female, black and white, young and old, rich and poor. What are we to do with the Spirit we receive? We are to go and share with others the wonderful salvation found in Christ Jesus.

My own personal call to the ministry came as a surprise to me. I was not expecting the Lord to use me because I did not realize God used women in the ministry.

At the time of my call I was still in the medical profession. I had been filled with the Holy Spirit and because of the tremendous transformation in my own life, I was eager to share with others this beautiful blessing. I had known the Lord since the age of twelve. However, I had not known Him in the power of the Holy Spirit. After my baptism in the Holy Spirit, I found I had a new holy boldness that I had not had before. I found myself witnessing and sharing with all who would listen. I wanted them to know of my new joy, love, peace and faith. I did not intend to pursue the path of becoming a female preacher. (I really did not know such existed). I just found myself preaching.

Actually all of us who know Christ should be "preachers." Preaching is simply sharing the good news of Jesus Christ. The clergy should not be the ones who do all the preaching; this is the responsibility of every member of the body of Christ.

When the Lord spoke to me about His plan for my life, I immediately thought of many objections. My first was that I was a woman, so how could He use me? I told Him I didn't have the kind of tremendous testimony that would cause people to listen to me. He said, "Betty, it is not your testimony that will cause people to listen, but it will be My Spirit and My anointing." He then ministered to me in a beautiful way to show me in His Word that it was Scriptural for women to minister. Most of these truths are in this book.

Our confusion over women ministering comes by misunderstanding the full counsel of God's Word. The verse with which this chapter begins is one of the first He revealed to me, "...there is neither male nor female..." in the Spirit. In heaven there will be no sex; so if we are walking in the Spirit now, we will not be conscious of sex, but only of the Spirit of God.

For in the resurrection they neither marry, nor are given in marriage, but are as the angels of God in heaven (Matthew 22:30).

If the Spirit of God is speaking through anyone, male or female, we should listen. We should also be able to discern when flesh is speaking. There are many prophetesses who spoke God's words recorded in the Bible. Mary and Elizabeth both prophesied in the first chapter of Luke.

Luke 2:36-38 records another woman who was a prophetess, **And there was one Anna, a prophetess, the daughter of Phanuel, of the tribe of Aser: she was of a great age, and had lived with a husband seven years from her virginity; And she was a widow of about fourscore and four years, which departed not from the temple, but served God with fastings and prayers night and day. And she coming in that instant gave thanks likewise unto the Lord, and spake of him to all them that looked for redemption in Jerusalem.**

This woman of God was supported by the temple as she lived there; she spoke to all who were looking for redemption (this would include men and women). God was certainly using her in a leadership position.

Another well-known prophetess in the Bible is Deborah. We find her story in Judges 4 and 5. She was a married woman who judged the entire nation of Israel. She certainly was in a leadership position, and her being a woman did not prevent God from using her. Under her leadership, Barak, her army captain, won a battle for the Lord.

There are many other prophetesses recorded in the Bible, but these accounts are sufficient for us to see that God does use women in this important office. (There is a difference between a woman or man being in the office of a prophet and moving in the simple gift of prophecy. The office of a prophet is a leadership position while the gift of prophecy is for the whole body.)

Office of Evangelist

The next office listed in **Ephesians 4:11** is that of the evangelist. Our present-day evangelists, for the most part, do not resemble the New Testament evangelists who were always anointed with the charismatic gifts and the power of the Holy Spirit. Miracles and healing were common under the ministries of those evangelists.

Philip is a good example as he was healing the sick, casting out demons and working miracles. **Then Philip went down to the city of Samaria, and preached Christ unto them. And the people with one accord gave heed unto those things which Philip spake, hearing and seeing the miracles which he did. For unclean spirits, crying with loud voice, came out of many that were possessed with them: and many taken with palsies, and that were lame, were healed. And there was great joy in that city (Acts 8:5-8).**

This same kind of anointing is resting on many handmaidens of the Lord today as the Lord is using them to bring forth healing and miracles. The late Kathryn Kuhlman is only one woman of many whom He has used as an evangelist. Many Spirit-filled women missionaries are also examples of God calling women to this ministry.

Office of Pastor

Another ministry is that of the pastor, or "shepherd," called by God. Other names for this office are "elder" and "bishop."

The present-day ministry of pastor is far from the Biblical example. So many pastors today are functioning in the role of a religious administrator with an office and staff having the oversight of a complex institution and organization, instead of giving themselves to the Word and prayer. This is not God's divine order

19

but a man-made system. In the Word of God we find many "elders" or "pastors" who ministered to new converts, assisting them in their growth in the Lord. The early-day church met in homes in small groups with elders or pastors present to oversee the meetings. The church was not a building as it has become today in the minds of many people, but rather a meeting of the saints to worship, study and fellowship. We can have church when only a small group are present who are seeking God. **For where two or three are gathered together in my name, there am I in the midst of them (Matthew 18:20).**

We find a pair of pastors and teachers who were a husband-and-wife team spoken of by Paul in **Romans 16**. This man and woman were co- workers with Paul in preaching the gospel and ministering to the church. In fact, they had a church in their home in which they pastored. **Greet Priscilla and Aquila my helpers in Christ Jesus: Who have for my life laid down their own necks: unto whom not only I give thanks, but also all the churches of the Gentiles. Likewise greet the church that is in their house... (Romans 16:3-5a).** The Lord is using many husband-wife teams today just as He used this couple in the New Testament.

My husband and I have been privileged to serve in this capacity. It's rewarding to allow the Holy Spirit to minister through us as He sees fit. We only want to be those vessels who stand ready for the Master's use. The Lord uses Bud to relate to many that I could not reach, and He uses me to minister to others that he could not reach. Together we are able to accomplish much more for the Lord. We are grateful that the Lord called us into His service.

Many women have not known that they can minister alongside their husbands, so they have stepped back in fear of displeasing God simply because they have been wrongly taught that women cannot hold an office ministry nor be in a leadership position. God is liberating these women today so that they can stand in equality with their husbands before the Lord, not putting the spotlight on

20

either one of them, but solely on the Lord. He is the one who is to be lifted up, not man, whether male or female.

Office of Teacher

The last office listed in **Ephesians 4:11** is that of the teacher. This is perhaps the most controversial ministry as far as women are concerned because of two Scriptures that seem to contradict others in the Word of God. However, if we look at these the Holy Spirit will clarify them so they do not become stumbling blocks for women teachers.

Let your women keep silence in the churches: for it is not permitted unto them to speak; but they are commanded to be under obedience, as also saith the law. And if they will learn anything, let them ask their husbands at home: for it is a shame for women to speak in the church (I Corinthians 14:34-35).

Some people have accused Paul of not being very fond of women because of this admonition. This is far from the truth as he commends several women in chapter 16 of Romans. **I commend unto you Phebe our sister, which is a servant of the church which is at Cenchrea: That ye receive her in the Lord, as becometh saints, and that ye assist her in whatsoever business she hath need of you: for she hath been a succourer of many, and of myself also (Romans 16:1-2).** Phebe was a minister or deaconess in this church, as the Greek word for servant here means "one who ministers or serves." Paul also says, **Salute Tryphena and Tryphosa, who labour in the Lord. Salute the beloved Persis, which laboured much in the Lord (Romans 16:12).** These were women who were laboring and ministering for the Lord.

Paul is not being prejudiced against women when he instructs the Corinthian women to keep silence. By looking at this entire chapter in Corinthians we find that Paul is dealing with problems

21

of disorder in the church. One of those problems was the fact that some women had not yet learned "church manners." In the early church the seating arrangement was quite different from our modern day churches. Men were seated on one side of the church while the women and children were seated on the opposite side. This is still practiced in Eastern cultures today. We saw this in the churches in India while on our last missionary journey there.

The women of Christ's day were generally uneducated and only the men were privileged with an education. Due to this situation, when the church met the women were tempted to shout across the room and ask their husbands the meaning of whatever was being taught. This disturbed the service. Paul was simply saying during the service, "Women, keep your children quiet and you be quiet, and if you have anything to ask your husbands, wait until you get home."

This certainly was not in reference to women speaking or teaching in the church, for we find in **I Corinthians 11:5** that women were praying and prophesying in the church. **I Corinthians 14:31** also says, **For ye may *all* prophesy one by one, that *all* may learn, and *all* may be comforted** (emphasis mine). All of the men and women could prophesy so that all of the men and women could learn. For someone to learn something, someone must be teaching.

Women can teach men as long as they are under the Holy Spirit's unction, for then it will be His Spirit teaching through them. If she is unlearned and unruly, as some of these Corinthian women were, then she should keep quiet until she can learn submission and the ways of the Lord. Women, however, who have been called of God, as Priscilla was in the New Testament, will not hesitate to teach whomever the Lord instructs them to teach.

Apollos was a well-known evangelist in the New Testament, and we find Priscilla and her husband instructing and teaching him a more perfect way.

And a certain Jew named Apollos, born at Alexandria, an eloquent man, and mighty in the scriptures, came to

22

Ephesus. This man was instructed in the way of the Lord; and being fervent in the spirit, he spake and taught diligently the things of the Lord, knowing only the baptism of John. And he began to speak boldly in the synagogue: whom when Aquila and Priscilla had heard, they took him unto them, and expounded unto him the way of God more perfectly (Acts 18:24-26).

Apollos was a mighty preacher who was preaching salvation through Christ, but he had not yet understood the baptism in the Holy Spirit. He only knew the baptism of John. Priscilla and Aquila took him aside and taught him in a more perfect way.

One other portion of Scripture that has kept women from rising to their rightful place in the church is **I Timothy 2:11-15** which says, **Let the woman learn in silence with all subjection. But I suffer not a woman to teach, nor to usurp authority over the man, but to be in silence. For Adam was first formed, then Eve. And Adam was not deceived, but the woman being deceived was in the transgression. Notwithstanding she shall be saved in childbearing, if they continue in faith and charity and holiness with sobriety.**

The point that Paul was trying to make in these verses was that wives were to be submissive in the home. In speaking of women here, he was referring to wives who had not yet learned the lesson of submission. It does not refer to all women.

Women who are called of God to a ministry already will have learned and applied this truth in their lives, or else the Lord would not have called them.

Just as the Scripture, **And be not drunk with wine, wherein is excess; but be filled with the Spirit (Ephesians 5:18),** does not apply to those who do not drink, even so it is with the above Scripture regarding usurping authority over men. If a woman does not usurp authority and try to boss her husband and other men, then this Scripture would not apply to her any more than "be not drunk with wine..." would apply to someone who did not drink.

Women Redeemed From the Curse

In the physical union of man and woman, God placed man as the head, even as Adam was the head of Eve. However, in the spirit each of them is responsible to God. No man can obtain salvation for his wife. She must come to God on her own. In chapter 3 of Genesis we find that the Lord gave both the man and woman certain penalties for their disobedience. These penalties were part of the curse that entered the earth as a result of their sin. **Unto the woman he said, I will greatly multiply thy sorrow and thy conception; in sorrow thou shalt bring forth children; and thy desire shall be to thy husband, and he shall rule over thee (Genesis 3:16).** Christ's death and resurrection redeemed man from the curse so that we no longer have to accept those things that sin produced. Women can rise above the curse and be restored to their original position of authority given them in the beginning before the fall. That position was one of equality with the husband.

So God created man in his own image, in the image of God created he him; male and female created he them. And God blessed them, and God said unto them, Be fruitful, and multiply, and replenish the earth, and subdue it: and have dominion over the fish of the sea, and over the fowl of the air, and over every living thing that moveth upon the earth (Genesis 1:27-28).

Ruling and Reigning in Christ

Here we see the command to have dominion over and subdue the earth was given to both Adam and Eve. They were both to rule and reign over the Lord's creation. The very act of subduing something requires authority, aggressiveness and leadership.

Within God's own nature we find these same qualities. We

are to become like Him as we are conformed to His image. Since this is true, there are times that under the unction of the Holy Spirit a woman should assert herself boldly. This assertion, however, should not be toward her husband, but rather toward the enemy, Satan. For women to become overcomers they must have this boldness and authority over the devil. God still desires that His people rule and reign with Him. His intention is to qualify us for that position, whether we be male or female. **And hath made us kings and priests unto God and his Father; to him be glory and dominion for ever and ever. Amen (Revelation 1:6).**

Does the Lord mean only the male sex will become kings and priests? No, even though "kings" is a masculine term, this is the ultimate destination He desires for all of His people. God has both a masculine and feminine nature. The mother heart of Jesus was evident as he prayed over Jerusalem. **O Jerusalem, Jerusalem, thou that killest the prophets, and stonest them which are sent unto thee, how often would I have gathered thy children together, even as a hen gathereth her chickens under her wings, and ye would not! (Matthew 23:37).** Submission is a feminine trait. However, Jesus submitted to the cross under the direction of the Father. If we walk in the Spirit, we too will possess both the masculine aggressiveness and feminine submissiveness of God.

The church has more women in it than men because of their natural inclination towards submission. This enables them to submit to God more easily. There are more male preachers than women because of their inherent boldness and aggressiveness. In the world, Satan has distorted the natural traits of many men and women through the sin of homosexuality. Homosexuality counterfeits and perverts the true image of man. God's nature is purity and all that is defilement is an abomination to Him.

Going back to **I Timothy 2:15**, we see that God's plan was for the natural woman to continue in faith, charity, holiness and sobriety so that she would be saved in childbearing. This means that when she accepts the Lord's plan for her life, she will not have the sorrow (the Hebrew word for sorrow means grief) that was pronounced upon her as part of the curse, nor will she be under the domination of her husband. She will rise to rule with him. (She, of course, will be submissive to her husband as with any other member of the body of Christ. Most of the problems concerning a woman's place in the church could be resolved if we understood that a woman's role in the home is different from her role in the church). The first prophecy of Jesus coming to this earth to overcome Satan is recorded in **Genesis 3:15, And I will put enmity between thee (Satan) and the woman, and between thy seed and her seed; it shall bruise thy head, and thou shalt bruise his heel.** Woman would be saved indeed through childbearing, that is, by the birth of the divine Child, Jesus. The sentence that was placed upon Eve and womankind would not hinder her soul's salvation if she trusted in the work of Christ's atonement. Woman would not come under a man's headship, spiritually, as the Lord was to become her spiritual head.

Coverings

Recent teachings have gone forth that say a woman must be under a male's headship, or "covering," to be able to minister for the Lord. This has even been applied to women who are unmarried. These false teachings dictate they must be under the male leadership of some church if they are to speak or minister. This is far from the true teaching of God's Word. Deborah is a perfect example of a woman acting independently of a male's so-called "covering." As judge over Israel, she acted under the leadership of God and gave orders to Barak. She had a husband, but she did not receive her instructions from him, but directly from God **(Judges 4)**. (This is not negating being a part of a local church, but rather saying she may be the leader of a local church.)

Let us look at the Scripture that speaks about "coverings" and see what God's Word really says. The eleventh chapter of I

26

Corinthians has caused many problems for the church around the world. The teaching that all women must be spiritually "covered" by a male is not the only one that has emerged from this portion of Scripture. Others have taken these verses to mean that a woman must have her head covered with some sort of wrap, such as a scarf, while she is prophesying or ministering. In some nations, the churches still hold to this teaching, as do some churches here in the USA. Many of our traditional churches have a vestige of this teaching that has remained in the popular custom of women wearing hats to church on Sunday.

What is God's real meaning of these verses and what is the true "covering"? One way we can discern between false and true teaching is to examine the fruit of it. Does it bring freedom, or legalism and bondage? As we look at this Scripture, we must re-member to examine it in the light of God's total Word and not just these isolated verses.

But I would have you know, that the head of every man is Christ; and the head of the woman is the man; and the head of Christ is God. Every man praying or prophesying, having his head covered, dishonoureth his head. But every woman that prayeth or prophesieth with her head uncovered dishonoureth her head: for that is even all one as if she were shaven. For if the woman be not covered, let her also be shorn: but if it be a shame for a woman to be shorn or shaven, let her be covered. For a man indeed ought not to cover his head, forasmuch as he is the image and glory of God: but the woman is the glory of the man. For the man is not of the woman; but the woman of the man. Neither was the man created for the woman; but the woman for the man. For this cause ought the woman to have power on her head because of the angels. Nevertheless neither is the man without the woman, neither the woman without the man, in the Lord. For as the woman is of the man, even so is the man also by the woman; but all things of God. Judge in yourselves: is it comely that a woman pray unto God uncovered? Doth not even nature itself teach

you, that, if a man hath long hair, it is a shame unto him? But if a woman have long hair, it is a glory to her: for her hair is given her for a covering. But if any man seem to be contentious, we have no such custom, neither the churches of God (I Corinthians 11:3-16). For the sake of clarity we will deal with this passage verse by verse.

First, we need to understand why this chapter was written. Paul had received a letter from the Corinthian church regarding many problems it was encountering. This epistle was written to help straighten out some confusing issues. One of these was the question of whether a woman should veil, or cover, her head in church since the custom was that most women kept their heads covered in and out of the church. The reason this was a much discussed issue was that one of the oral Jewish traditions dictated that when entering the temple for worship, the males, or "heads of the house," were to wear the Jewish tallith, or veil. According to the Jewish tradition this was a sign of reverence toward God and a condemnation of sin. Paul was very strongly against all Jewish legalism (circumcision being one of these) being imposed on new Christian converts. He was also opposed to the veiling or covering of men because they were no longer under any condemnation or guilt since Jesus took that away through His sacrifice.

Now the question had come up over women veiling or covering in church. What would he say for them to do? Paul seized the opportunity to teach them by presenting a spiritual analogy that would enable them to arrive at their own conclusion. We find Paul's conclusion to their question of women veiling in **verse 16**, **But if any man seem to be contentious, we have no such custom, neither the churches of God**. He simply says this is a custom of the women, but it is not a church ordinance. This explanation clarifies the matter for us today, but we will miss a beautiful spiritual application if we fail to look at these verses further as every portion of the Scriptures contains some deep and eternal principle applicable to every age. We can see that Paul is using an analogy here. He is not discussing a cloth covering, or veil, when

28

he speaks of a woman having her head covered, because in **verse 15** he clearly says a woman's hair is given to her for a covering. **But if a woman have long hair, it is a glory to her: for her hair is given her for a covering.**

What kind of covering does he mean? He is not speaking of a literal covering at all, but a spiritual covering. Let us see what this spiritual covering is. **Isaiah 30:1** says, **Woe to the rebellious children, saith the Lord, that take counsel, but not of me; and that cover with a covering, but not of my spirit, that they may add sin to sin.** We can see here that the Spirit of God is our covering. He warned those that sought any "covering" other than His Spirit. This should speak plainly to us that our covering is not to be found in men. Another verse that tells us about God's covering is **Psalm 104:1-2, Bless the Lord, O my soul. O Lord my God, thou art very great; thou art clothed with honour and majesty. Who coverest thyself with light as with a garment: who stretchest out the heavens like a curtain.** We see that God is covered in honour, majesty and light. Where light is, there is no darkness and evil; where honour is, there is truth.

The covering God is talking about is the Spirit of Truth and Light. With an understanding of this covering, we can now look at **verse 4 of I Corinthians 11** and see that it says, **Every man praying or prophesying, having his head covered, dishonoureth his head. Verse 3** tells us who his head is, **But I would have you know, that the head of every man is Christ; ...and the head of Christ is God.** If Christ is man's head and God is Christ's head, then if the man covers Jesus so that the light of God cannot be seen in Him, it is a dishonor for Christ. The Bible speaks that we are to let our light shine, not to cover it.

Ye are the light of the world. A city that is set on an hill cannot be hid. Neither do men light a candle, and put it under a bushel, but on a candlestick; and it giveth light unto all that are in the house. Let your light so shine before men, that they may see your good works, and glorify your Father which is in heaven (Matthew 5:14-16). If men are going to prophesy, pray and minister in the church, then they are not to dishonor their head, Jesus. They must let the light of God shine through them. Men are not to "cover" God's glory and majesty, but let it come forth from them. This light will go forth with truth and honor.

In the Old Testament it was a shame for men to cover their heads; that is why the Jewish tallith was worn (to represent the shame and guilt of their sins). Jeremiah speaks of men covering their heads because of their shame. **Because the ground is chapt, for there was no rain in the earth, the plowmen were ashamed, they covered their heads (Jeremiah 14:4)**. Whenever men do not allow Christ to flow out of them, but cover their head, Christ, it is a shame. Men do not have to defend their position as long as Christ is flowing from them, as Jesus will "cover" for them. They don't have to "cover" for Him. The Lord will justify those that are shining for Him. The Lord's mercy, love, kindness and goodness should be evident in those men who are in the ministry. They will be gentle to their wives, considerate and loving if they are truly letting God shine through them. Christ is the man's head and should not be covered, or it will bring dishonor to the Lord.

Now what about women? **I Corinthians 11:5** says, **But every woman that prayeth or prophesieth with her head uncovered dishonoureth her head: for that is even all one as if she were shaven.** Who is the married woman's matrimonial head? Of course, her husband, the man. Now the list in verse 3 is not a chain of command because although God is at the top He shares His glory equally with Jesus, even though He is His head. The same should be true in the marriage relationship. If a man is truly the "head" after the pattern of Christ, he will support and lift his wife up to his own level of authority. The true "headship" is won by self- sacrificing love which is how Christ won His Church, not by rule and domination. The woman's head is to be "covered." How does she cover her head, that is, her husband? One way she is to cover him is by the words of her mouth.

David realized that the words we speak produce a blessing or a curse. **Psalm 140:7 and 9** says, **O God the Lord, the strength**

of my salvation, thou hast covered my head in the day of battle...As for the head of those that compass me about, let the mischief of their own lips cover them. If a woman's lips do not confess the Word of God and truth, she will be "uncovering" her head. If a woman tears her husband down with ugly and degrading words, and her lips speak negative things against him, she will find in her "day of battle" she will not be covered by the Lord. David was covered because he spoke those things pleasing to the Lord.

Women who pray or minister in public should not degrade their husbands in their private lives as this is a shame before the Lord. It brings shame to their matrimonial "heads." Women should not uncover their "heads" as the Scripture says it would be the same if she were to go about with her head shaven. No woman would purposely shave her head, yet women are doing this spiritually when they expose their husband's faults, malign them or degrade them in any way. We are to cover our husband's weaknesses, not "uncover" them. There is a story in the Old Testament about Noah that shows us how displeased God is when His men are exposed and not covered.

And Noah began to be an husbandman, and he planted a vineyard: And he drank of the wine, and was drunken; and he was uncovered within his tent. And Ham, the father of Canaan, saw the nakedness of his father, and told his two brothers without. And Shem and Japheth took a garment, and laid it upon both their shoulders, and went backward, and covered the nakedness of their father; and their faces were backward, and they saw not their father's nakedness. And Noah awoke from his wine, and knew what his younger son had done unto him. And he said, Cursed be Canaan; a servant of servants shall he be unto his brethren. And he said, Blessed be the Lord God of Shem; and Canaan shall be his servant. God shall enlarge Japheth, and he shall dwell in the tents of Shem; and Canaan shall be his servant (Genesis 9:20-27).

Noah's son, Ham, discovered his father's nakedness, but instead of covering him, he went and told his two brothers. Shem and Japheth not only refused to look on their father in his exposed state, but covered him as well.

As wives, we should cover our husband's faults and failures, not expose them to others. It's a shame to leave our "heads uncovered." We know that because man and wife are one flesh, for either of them to hurt or expose the other, it is the same as if they were doing it to themselves. We can see that after Noah discovered what had happened, he pronounced a curse upon the son of Ham (Canaan) and a blessing upon Shem and Japheth. When wives uncover their husband's nakedness, they actually bring a curse against their heads and their marriages. A woman cannot talk about her husband without it affecting her because she, in essence, is talking about herself. If women expect God to bless their marriages, then they must "cover" their heads. A woman who is guilty of exposing her husband becomes uncovered too. The Lord cannot bless her with His anointing when she walks out uncovered by God. Husbands and wives are to lay their lives down for each other.

Sin of Divorce

In today's society divorce is the way out of an unpleasant situation. Instead of suffering on behalf of a mate who is out of God's will, more Christians are beginning to take this easy way out. This sin has even taken place in so-called Spirit-filled ministers. Those parties who seek divorce instead of sacrifice cannot expect God to bless their ministries. He cannot continue to anoint ministers who have no grief in their hearts for their mates. They actually are destroying their own flesh. Of course, there are many innocent mates who do not desire their marriages dissolved, but at their mates' insistence God's Word says they must release them. **But if the unbelieving depart, let him depart. A brother or a**

sister is not under bondage in such cases: but God hath called us to peace (I Corinthians 7:15).

Not only should we not expose our mates, but this same mercy and compassion should be shown towards every member in the body of Christ. We, as Christians, should cover one another's sins, not expose them. We should resist gossip as we would resist any other sin. We should ask for God's love for those who are fallen.

There is a rampant spirit of division in the earth today that is seeking to destroy not only marriages, but all of our relationships. We must recognize this attack of the enemy and resist it. The Scripture in I Corinthians 11 is written concerning men and women who are ministering in the church as it speaks of those who are praying and prophesying. We cannot expect our prayers to be answered if we do not have a proper relationship with our mates.

Likewise, ye husbands, dwell with them according to knowledge, giving honour unto the wife, as unto the weaker vessel, and as being heirs together of the grace of life; that your prayers be not hindered. Finally, be ye all of one mind, having compassion one of another, love as brethren, be pitiful, be courteous: Not rendering evil for evil, or railing for railing: but contrariwise blessing: knowing that ye are thereunto called, that ye should inherit a blessing. For he that will love life, and see good days, let him refrain his tongue from evil, and his lips that they speak no guile: Let him eschew evil, and do good; let him seek peace and ensue it. For the eyes of the Lord are over the righteous, and his ears are open unto their prayers: but the face of the Lord is against them that do evil (I Peter 3:7-12).

Ministries of Married Men and Women

Women ministers who seek their ministries at the expense of their husbands' are not in God's order. If a woman steps on her husband and family to go forth in a ministry, she will not have one for long. If the Lord truly desires for her to have a ministry, He will deal with her husband as she seeks God. God will put it in the husband's heart to accept that which He is requiring of her. The most important thing is not to move in the gifts and a ministry, but to have the virtue of Christ in one's life. If a person has a world-wide ministry but his marriage and family have been destroyed through divorce, he really has gained nothing for the Lord. How heartbreaking to come before the Lord and not be able to present Him those in our families because of our failure to minister to them. Saving the whole world while losing our own family would not count with the Lord. He is a God of order, and if He calls a man and woman to minister for Him, He will not do it at the expense of a marriage and children. If God truly calls us, He will expand our hearts and strength to maintain both our homes and our ministries.

Of course, the other extreme would be to refuse to follow the Lord when He calls because of family. We must be willing to leave all when we know that it is the Lord. However, should God require that, He would always have us make provision for our families and never neglect them. Either they would go with us, or He would provide others to care for those children that needed to stay behind. The most important thing we should do is be sure that it is God calling us and not just our desire to go out and evangelize. We can tell if it is God by the fruit it is producing in our lives and our families. We should be sure our children are covered by God's Spirit through prayer regardless if we are full-time ministers, or if we are called to the ministry of a mother and housewife.

The Lord desires to use each member in families in His great plan. Husbands and wives can have powerful ministries as they submit to God and each other. They need one another and should be dependent upon each other. Women praying and prophesying need the power of their husband's covering and love over them as the angels of God are present in a greater way when both are serving the Lord. The two together can do a mighty work for the Lord. **Neither was the man created for the woman; but the woman for the man. For this cause ought the woman to have power on her head because of the angels. Nevertheless neither is the man without the woman, neither the woman without the man, in the Lord (I Corinthians 11:9-11).**

This teaching was meant for those husbands and wives who minister in the church. In no way is it directed to those ministers who are single. They need no man's covering as the true covering is God. If they are following God they will be covered by Him. In fact, we can all cover one another with our prayers. We need not think we must be subject to some man's covering in order to minister. We need one another and are covered by one another as the Holy Spirit directs our prayers for each other. But, we need no other man's permission to be obedient to God and do the things He speaks for us to do. Whether we are married or single the Lord will cover us as He calls us to follow Him.

Celibacy and the Ministry

Some people, having a desire to please God, think that the only way for them to have a successful ministry is to remain single, just as the apostle Paul did. Even though they have a strong desire to marry, they feel they could serve the Lord better alone. This is only true if their desire does not leave a weak area in their lives exposed to Satan. If they are being continually tempted in that weak area by relationships with the opposite sex, it would be better if they were married. Paul tells us the same thing in his epistle to the Corinthians. **I say therefore to the unmarried and widows, It is good for them if they abide even as I. But if they cannot contain, let them marry: for it is better to marry than to burn (I Corinthians 7:8-9).** Paul was not saying in this chapter that celibacy was better than marriage, but that it was better for him and was acceptable for others because it could free people

35

to give of themselves more wholeheartedly to the Lord. Of course, this would only be true if they were as satisfied as Paul was to be single.

Since marriage was God's original plan for man, the Bible had to also establish that celibacy was acceptable and pleasing to the Lord. He leaves this choice up to us as individuals. God does not force someone to remain alone to please Him, nor does He force one to marry. We must choose what we desire. If we should desire to marry, we must allow the Lord to provide the right mate who will not interfere with His plan for us. When we allow the Lord to send the right person to be our mate, that one will enhance our lives. The Bible says, **Marriage is honourable in all, and the bed undefiled: but whoremongers and adulterers God will judge (Hebrews 13:4)**.

In **I Timothy 3:1-7** and **Titus 1:5-10** we see the qualifications of bishops (pastors). A bishop or pastor should be the husband of one wife, rule his household well, and have his children well disciplined. This certainly does not show that he wanted all ministers to be celibates, or Paul would have told Titus and Timothy to find unmarried men for this responsible position in the church. The devil whispers to some that they can be more spiritual without a mate, and if the persons are married, many times they divorce believing this lie. Others who are single remain unmarried, but are secretly miserable as they believe God is asking them to be a martyr.

This martyr complex keeps many people from enjoying their relationship with Christ because they see Him as an austere God who denies all physical pleasure. The Lord wants us to be joyful and happy, and He does not mind our enjoying any good thing as long as it does not come between Him and us.

Choosing a Mate

There are other single people who are constantly out looking for a mate, and they're so miserable because God has not sent them one. They have prayed and prayed, yet they still have no mate. Some settle for Satan's provision instead of asking God for the patience to wait for the one whom God would send.

The majority of these are women looking for men. If they would look to Jesus and seek to please Him, rather than being concerned about a mate, soon they would find the right one crossing their path. Looking for a man to keep them from being lonely, to fill their needs or to be a father to their children is not solely the right reason for desiring a husband. Some women are still much in the flesh and need the Lord to purge them from their selfish desires. They should ask the Lord to fill them with His love and peace. They need to be concerned about what kind of wife they would be for a husband.

Being single is a wonderful time for the Lord to prepare us for a marriage. As we can seek God to cleanse us of the world and help us become the kind of mate that would bless someone, we would soon find we were not lonely. First, the Lord would begin using us to bless others; then we would find we are content in Him. Eventually, in God's plan and timing, He would bless us with a wonderful husband so that both of our lives could be a witness for Him. If a marriage cannot glorify the Lord, then it would be better to remain alone. There are worse things than being alone. One of these is to be out of God's will by compromising and marrying someone who does not feel the same way we do toward the Lord.

Marriage is the second major choice we make in our lives, and we should never enter into it without much prayer. To rush into a marriage can be disastrous. The most important decision of our lives, of course, is our decision to follow the Lord. This decision is not a one-time declaration, but a daily determination to follow Jesus above all. Women, by nature being more emotional than men, are very susceptible to the enemy leading them astray through a man. This area of the flesh should be brought under the Lord's subjection so that Satan does not get the advantage and consequently destroy their lives and ministries. So many have failed the Lord because they chose a man or woman over the Lord.

We find this true throughout the Bible, too. Solomon's heathen wives led him into idolatry. Samson lost his eyes because of a woman, Delilah. David committed murder because of passion for Bathsheba.

Our emotions need to be cleansed as they are not the sign of love. The true definition of love is "God is love." If God is not in a relationship it is not love; but lust. What this world calls love is really lust since it is built on what the other person does for me, not what I can do for him or her. If the other person fails to keep up his end of the bargain, a divorce occurs because the offended mate is no longer pleased. This is the attitude of the world's so-called "love." God's love loves without receiving back; God's love is forgiving and patient. God's love is gentle and kind. God's love waits. God's love sacrifices.

I Corinthians 13 gives us a beautiful definition of real love. Man's emotions are not a reliable gauge upon which to establish a marriage relationship. We must know in the Spirit that it is God's will. It is much better to marry for character than for emotion. Emotions fluctuate; character doesn't. Emotions are in the soulish realm, and unless the carnal mind has been renewed, Satan can give us emotions or feelings of love for someone of his choosing. (If he did not have this in his power, he could not split up marriages.) One of his favorite techniques is to suddenly take away the feelings one once had for his mate and give feelings for someone else. When he has successfully convinced a person that he no longer loves his mate, then he leads him to divorce, whispering, "You are living a lie." After he has destroyed that marriage, he then leads one to marry again by stirring his emotions for another.

Then, an unexpected thing happens. Before too long, friction begins to develop with the new mate, then arguing. Finally, he finds the same thing has happened again; he feels no emotion for his new mate and the next divorce is in the making. "Falling in love" is Satan's way. The very expression of these words should tell us something. A Christian should not "fall" into any trap.

Marriage, in a Christian's life, should be based on a decision directed by the Holy Spirit. A Christian's love for another is a commitment. Of course, the Lord will supply the emotions for the mate He sends, but that should not be the criterion for making the decision to marry. The Lord should be sought, and whatever He speaks to us we should do. He knows the future and what is best for us. If we trust Him He will not fail us in this or any other important area. Women or men who allow emotions to rule them will never be victorious Christians. Emotions should always follow, never lead.

During Old and New Testament times, fathers and mothers chose the mates for their children. God's people were very careful to choose those who were "believers." We find this practice still prevalent in India and other Eastern cultures. The parents, being older and more prudent, made wiser decisions than the children in this area. The divorce rate in India is only about 7%, whereas in our country at the present it is nearing 50%. Marriages that are loveless can be saved and restored simply by asking God to restore the love that was once there. Sexual relationships can also be healed by praying for a desire for one's mate. Prayer is a mighty weapon. God's love can mend and heal, providing people are willing to lay down their lives for their mates. His love will not fade, as does the love of the world.

Those who are single and have never been married are cautioned in God's Word to seek a mate who is a like believer. **Be ye not unequally yoked together with unbelievers: for what fellowship hath righteousness with unrighteousness? and what communion hath light with darkness? (II Corinthians 6:14)**. Many precious people suffer because they are living with unsaved mates. Some did not have Christ when they made their marriage decision, but they have since found the Lord. Those will have God's grace and love to win their mates for Jesus. The Lord always strives to bring the lost mate to Himself through the partner who knows Him. Mighty miracles of deliverance and salvation have occurred when people have endured suffering in order to bring their mates to the Lord. Those people who have the light, but choose to marry into darkness by yoking themselves to un-saved mates find that their flesh has led them away from God.

The Lord wants to bless marriage unions and see His plans fulfilled in both mates' lives. What a glorious plan He had from the beginning for both male and female. The fruit of a physical marriage is children. (Our spiritual marriage with Jesus should produce fruit also. Others are born into God's kingdom because of our love for the Lord as the fruit of the Holy Spirit becomes evident in our lives.)

Problems of Divorce

Instead of marriages being blessed and fulfilled, we are see-ing more and more people end up in the divorce court because of Satan's work of division in homes across this nation.

It is understandable how those outside of Christ end up with broken homes, but how sad it is that now Satan is even destroying Spirit-filled homes. Perhaps it is because we have not been taught how to overcome the enemy or die to self. Whatever the reasons, there are many who have suffered the trauma of divorce.

How are we to deal with those who have suffered in this area? We see so many extremes being taught on this subject that it is difficult to have the proper perspective of this problem in the church.

First we must call divorce what it is -- sin. Then we must look to God's Word to see how He deals with this, or any other sin. Divorce causes one to commit the sin of adultery.

It hath been said, Whosoever shall put away his wife, let him give her a writing of divorcement: But I say unto you, That whosoever shall put away his wife, saving for the cause of fornication, causeth her to commit adultery: and whoso-

**ever shall marry her that is divorced committeth adultery
(Matthew 5:31-32).**

Now let us look at a case concerning a woman who was
caught in the act of adultery and see how the Lord deals with her.

**They say unto him, Master, this woman was taken in
adultery, in the very act. Now Moses in the law commanded
us, that such should be stoned: but what sayest thou? This
they said, tempting him, that they might have to accuse him,
But Jesus stooped down, and with his finger wrote on the
ground, as though he heard them not. So when they continued asking him, he lifted up himself, and said unto them, He
that is without sin among you, let him first cast a stone at her.
And again he stooped down, and wrote on the ground. And
they which heard it, being convicted by their own conscience,
went out one by one, beginning at the eldest, even unto the
last: and Jesus was left alone, and the woman standing in the
midst. When Jesus had lifted up himself, and saw none but
the woman, he said unto her, Woman, where are those thine
accusers? hath no man condemned thee? She said, No man,
Lord. And Jesus said unto her, Neither do I condemn thee:
go, and sin no more (John 8:4-11).**

From this account we see the Lord extending mercy to this
woman and forgiving her of her sin. We also notice that He made
an important statement, "He that is without sin among you, let
him first cast a stone."

The Lord treats all sins alike as far as redemption is concerned; sin is sin. The answer to every sin problem is the accep-
tance of Jesus and His sacrifice that cleanses us from sin. If we
turn to Jesus, no matter what sin we commit, we will find forgiveness and mercy. The Lord did not say she had not sinned, but
forgave her and admonished her to "sin no more." The sin of divorce is not the unpardonable sin. No matter what sin we have
committed in our lives, whether it be lying, cheating, stealing,
murder or divorce, Jesus made a way for us to cleansed and forgiven. When the Lord forgives sin, He also ceases to remember it.

God's love and forgiveness is so different from man's. **Hebrews 10:17** says, **And their sins and iniquities will I remember no more.**

What About Remarriage?

Yes, divorce is a sin. We can plainly see the damage it does to the lives of all involved. It is straight from the pit of hell. Yet, there is hope and forgiveness for the divorcee. Satan often lies and tells people that God is doing the separating, but it is not God. God is not the author of divorce. However, His Word does give instructions to those whose unbelieving mates desire a divorce.

And the woman which hath an husband that believeth not, and if he be pleased to dwell with her, let her not leave him. For the unbelieving husband is sanctified by the wife, and the unbelieving wife is sanctified by the husband: else were your children unclean; but now are they holy. But if the unbelieving depart, let him depart. A brother or a sister is not under bondage in such cases: but God hath called us to peace (I Corinthians 7:13-15).

If this happens, the mate that is left is not under any bondage to this marriage. He is free to remarry should the Lord lead him to do so.

Much conflict about Christians remarrying has arisen in the church because of Jesus' words in **Matthew 19:3-9,**

The Pharisees also came unto him, tempting him, and saying unto him, Is it lawful for a man to put away his wife for every cause? And he answered and said unto them, Hath ye not read, that he which made them at the beginning made them male and female, And said, For this cause shall a man leave father and mother, and shall cleave to his wife: and they twain shall be one flesh. Wherefore they are no more twain, but one flesh? What therefore God hath joined together, let

not man put asunder. They say unto him, Why did Moses then give a writing of divorcement, and to put her away? He saith unto them, Moses because of the hardness of your hearts suffered you to put away your wives: but from the beginning it was not so. And I say unto you, Whosoever shall put away his wife, except it be for fornication, and shall marry another, committeth adultery: and whoso marrieth her which is put away doth commit adultery. The Lord points out that those who divorce their mates have "hard hearts." God did not mean for divorce to happen. In the beginning His perfect will was for man and woman to remain married their entire lifetimes.

Does this statement of Jesus leave no room for remarriage? This verse has brought much bondage on those who have not looked at this Scripture in the light of the entire Word of God. First of all we must understand that the Pharisees here were attempting to trick Jesus into disagreeing with the Mosaic law so they could discount His ministry. Jesus knew this. Because the question asked here was in regard to divorce, Jesus quoted the perfect law concerning it. He, being perfect, could do no less. Had the Pharisees asked him, "Master, is it permissible to lie or steal?" He would have quoted the perfect law in regard to these sins. **Exodus 20:15-16, Thou shalt not steal. Thou shalt not bear false witness against thy neighbour.** Jesus also knew that man was not perfect and that man would fail, so other portions of His Word deal with the problem of sin. Man could not keep the perfect law; he failed. But the perfect God made a way for imperfect man to be forgiven of his sins through the blood of Jesus. Therefore, no matter what sins we have committed, we can find forgiveness and cleansing through Christ. He not only forgives the sin of divorce, but because of His perfect forgiveness, He forgets the sin and it becomes as if we had never committed it as far as He is concerned. Praise God! We have a new start in Christ as the old is wiped away.

The Lord has a compassionate heart and He wishes us to have the same attitude toward those who have committed this

43

sin. In fact, the Word of God deals with any transgression of the law as a serious offense. It matters not how big or little we might consider the sin to be. In God's eyes, sin is sin, and all sin must have the same remedy of Christ's cleansing. If we point our finger at other's sins without dealing with our own, we are bringing judgment upon ourselves.

For whosoever shall keep the whole law, and yet offend in one point, he is guilty of all. For he that said, Do not commit adultery, said also, Do not kill. Now if thou commit no adultery, yet if thou kill, thou art become a transgressor of the law. So speak ye, and so do, as they that shall be judged by the law of liberty. For he shall have judgment without mercy, that hath shewed no mercy; and mercy rejoiceth against judgment (James 2:10-13).

From this Scripture we see that if we commit that least sin (one point), we are still guilty of the whole law (murder, adultery, etc.) Therefore we should not judge those involved in the sins of divorce and adultery without mercy, or else we will be judged the same way. We could be judging others critically in this area while committing the same sin in our hearts.

One can commit adultery without divorcing his mate as this sin can be committed in the heart. **But I say unto you, That whosoever looketh on a woman to lust after her hath committed adultery with her already in his heart (Matthew 5:28)**. We are to minister to others compassionately in the area of divorce, for we have all sinned and fallen short of His perfection in many areas of our lives.

Can Divorced People Minister?

To ban people from ministering because they have suffered a divorce or to deny them the privilege of a Christian marriage is not in accordance with God's nature. If people have repented of their sin of divorce, then in God's eyes their sins are gone and forgotten. The true church will have the same compassion and understanding in its heart.

Some use the Scripture in **I Timothy 3:2** to disqualify those who have been married before from ever becoming an elder or bishop. **A bishop then must be blameless, the husband of one wife, vigilant, sober, of good behaviour, given to hospitality, apt to teach.** The reason for the specification of "one wife" here was that in Christ's day some were still practicing polygamy. Christ's teaching was calling people back to God's original plan of one man for one woman. In the Old Testament, polygamy had been introduced to God's people by the heathen nations and the Lord had to purge His people from this evil as well as one of "divorce for every cause." The hardness of man's heart had led him a long way from the intended purposes of God.

Now, we are warned in Scripture that we are not to use our liberty as a license to sin. **For, brethren, ye have been called unto liberty; only use not liberty for an occasion to the flesh, but by love serve one another (Galatians 5:13).** Those who would seek a divorce simply because they know God forgives would be committing willful sin and would have to face the consequences of that sin.

Those in bad marriages should not use divorce as an escape just because they are in an unpleasant situation, but should seek God for the healing of their relationship. The Lord desires to use such circumstances for redemptive purposes. He wants to heal and deliver the partner that is not committed to Him. This is perfect soil for the growth of the fruits of long-suffering (patience), faith and love to take place in the mate who is hurting due to lack of love in the marriage. God's kind of love can overcome in the situation, and a mighty miracle of healing can come to that marriage and home.

In divorces, children suffer as much as their parents. Emotional healings are needed for all who come out of split homes. God is healing and restoring those who seek His way. Those who continue in the world will only suffer more heartache until they allow the Lord to completely rule in their lives. God alone can "pick up the pieces" and put them together in a second marriage. Without God, a second marriage will only compound the existing problems. Men and women should seek God diligently in regard to this important step in their lives. Only by following God's plan and His Word will marriage be the fulfilling and beautiful relationship it was meant to be, regardless if it is a first or second marriage.

The Christian Wife

In **Titus 2:3-5**, women are given some instructions regarding their husbands, children and homes. **The aged women likewise, that they be in behaviour as becometh holiness, not false accusers, not given to much wine, teachers of good things; That they may teach the young women to be sober, to love their husbands, to love their children...that the word of God be not blasphemed.** One thing we notice about these verses is that the older women are instructed to teach the younger women how to love their husbands. In our society we have the idea that when we fall in love with a man, this love (emotion) will keep the marriage together. This is far from the truth. Of course, emotional love is part of marriage, but the kind of love that the Scripture is referring to here in these verses has to be taught and learned. It is God's love as spoken of in **I Corinthians 13**. We might also call it character.

The first step in learning how to love a husband, or anyone else for that matter, is to receive Christ into our hearts and let Him become our teacher. As we love Him and He loves us, that love spills over to those around us. We learn how to love others through reading, studying and applying God's Word to our hearts and our lives. Those who are older and more experienced can share with the younger ladies in order that they may be spared many heartaches by heeding their godly advice. Let us not think

46

that we have all the answers but truly be open to the advice of those who are older and wiser whether they be in the church, or part of our family. Remember, the first commandment with a promise is the one that says, **Honour thy father and thy mother: that thy days may be long upon the land which the Lord thy God giveth thee (Exodus 20:12).**

Even as small children, if we fail to obey our parents, our days can be shortened. For example, if a parent tells his child not to play in the street and he disobeys, he can be killed. God places elders as leaders and guides to help the younger Christians to mature. We need a submissive spirit to be able to learn from others.

A necessary ingredient for a compatible union, in spite of the abuses that occur when men are wrongly taught about their headship, is that women submit to their husbands. What does God expect of women in this area? First of all, we must understand that submission is an attitude and not just an action. Submission begins in the heart. There is a story about a little boy that was instructed by his teacher to sit down and be quiet. Because of his rebellious nature he did not want to do this, but was forced to by his teacher. Later, the children in the class were chiding him by saying, "Boy, you really sat down and shut up when the teacher approached you with the paddle." The rebellious boy replied, "I may have been sitting down on the outside, but I was still standing up on the inside."

Many times women who claim to be submissive are only outwardly going through the motions of submission while inwardly they are still resenting their position in life. A prayer of submission would be in order: "Father, help me to be content in the role you created me for and give me a submissive spirit, not only toward my mate, but also toward each member in the body of Christ. Let me serve and not expect to be served. Create within me a lamb-like spirit even as Christ our Lord had. Amen." Of course, as we have mentioned, there are limits to submission as it should always be "as unto the Lord." We must first submit to God and then the problems involving submission to others will be resolved by Him. Some results that can occur when women are not in a right relationship with men are divorce, rebellious children, emotional problems and sexual frigidity.

One of the main causes for these problems is an evil spiritual force of female domination. In **I Corinthians 11:3, Ephesians 5:22-25**, and **Ephesians 6:1-3**, the divine order for families is stated. The husband is the head, then the wife is second in command, with the children in obedience to them. When the woman seeks to usurp this authority and rule the home, havoc results and the home is left wide open for Satanic attack. **As for my people, children are their oppressors, and women rule over them. O my people, they which lead thee cause thee to err, and destroy the way of thy paths (Isaiah 3:12)**. In our land today, children are rebellious, causing strife in the homes, and women have become bossy and demanding. It is no wonder homes are falling apart. This type of spirit in a woman is a "Jezebel spirit." Just as Jezebel ruled her husband, King Ahab, in the Bible (**I Kings 21:25**), many women today are guilty of the same sin. This domineering and ruling spirit is not just found in women alone for we see it in men, too, when they use tyrannical means to rule their homes. The Lord would have our homes be examples of love, and the authority should be exercised in love. When someone has a "Jezebel spirit," it subtly manipulates the lives of everyone around him. Should we be guilty of this domineering spirit, let us ask the Lord to deliver us and create within us a sweet submissive spirit that is pleasing to the Lord. We will then be willing to listen to our husbands, knowing that the logic God gave man is for the protection of the woman.

Man's logic and ideas, coupled with a woman's sensitivity, blend to aid each other in making decisions. Learning to hear the voice of the Lord is one area where both husband and wife can confirm to each other what the Spirit is saying as they each seek the will of God on any given circumstance. The woman will usually have a certain inclination about it, while the man will have a definite idea regarding the situation. The ideal is, of course, for both husband and wife to walk totally submitted unto the Lord. When this is not the case, the woman should not disregard her husband's advice, for the Lord can and does speak through unsaved husbands. When the wife is submitted to the Lord, the Lord will deal with her husband. Extreme submission where the wife never offers advice to her husband, or is never allowed to think for herself, is out of balance as God did not intend any human being to be another's "door mat." This is an example of that domineering "Jezebel spirit." People under this kind of dominance need deliverance, as do the ones imposing their domineering spirit. The Lord wants every area and dimension of our lives to be balanced in Him.

Christian Duties of Wives and Mothers

Another area where Satan tries to push women to extremes is in keeping household duties and spiritual pursuits in balance. Women who are unequally yoked are especially vulnerable in this area. Perhaps you know women who serve their husbands "tapes for breakfast," "Charismatic book reviews for lunch," and "Praise-the-Lord's for dinner." If this is not done under the Holy Spirit's unction and with His wisdom, it can turn husbands away from, not toward the Lord. A change of diet might speak more loudly than incessant talking about Jesus. A neat house, nice meals, and a genuine interest in the husband and his interests many times speaks louder than all the tapes. To fulfill her household duties, a woman may have to give up some of her "spiritual" activities. Three meetings a week really do not make us spiritual anyway.

Real love is giving up what we would like to do in order to make another happy. We have all heard the old saying, "The way to a man's heart is through his stomach." If a wife has claimed her husband's heart for Jesus, she might try reaching it through his stomach, if all else has failed. Then, when he asks why the sudden change, she can humbly say the Lord spoke to her about neglecting him and the home, and that Jesus very much wants happy homes and happy husbands. He will be interested in knowing a God like that. It works with rebellious kids, too, applied a little differently. Many of our family members are really crying out for love through their very acts of rebellion. Let's remember to spend time with them, as God gave us the home first.

Some wives neglect their husbands and homes by engaging in too many spiritual pursuits. Of course, the opposite problem can also exist in our homes. Other problems arise when wives are so neat and fastidious about their homes that so much time is spent on cleaning and cooking that they neglect the much needed time of family worship and fellowship. Houses then become a "shrine" to be admired, placing more emphasis on the residence than the residents. Women can become "Marthas" instead of "Marys."

Now it came to pass, as they went, that he entered into a certain village: and a certain woman named Martha received him into her house. And she had a sister called Mary, which also sat at Jesus' feet, and heard his word. But Martha was cumbered about much serving, and came to him, and said, Lord, dost thou not care that my sister hath left me to serve alone? bid her therefore that she help me. And Jesus answered and said unto her, Martha, Martha, thou art careful and troubled about many things: But one thing is needful: and Mary hath chosen that good part, which shall not be taken away from her (Luke 10:38-42).

The Lord wants both areas balanced in our lives, so let us remember not to be so "heavenly minded" that we are no "earthly good." And on the other hand, let's not get so earthbound that we miss the beauty of the Spirit.

The woman has her primary responsibility in the home since the Scripture says she is to be the keeper of the home. **To be discreet, chaste, keepers at home, good, obedient to their own husbands, that the word of God be not blasphemed (Titus**

2:5). Preparing meals for the family is one of her prime duties. The world has set the standard when it comes to eating, rather than the Word of God. Here is another area where we need to be sensitive to the Holy Spirit's guidance. Besides seeing to it that each member receives spiritual food, the Lord is emphasizing to His people that they need to make changes in their physical diets and receive the proper natural foods. Most of God's people have experienced His healing hand in their bodies, but one problem that seems to be prevalent is that after receiving healing, the devil comes to rob them of God's gifts. If we exercise our faith and rebuke the enemy in the name of Jesus, he will flee. If, however, you have done this and are still experiencing illness, perhaps the problem is one of maintaining the gift God has given you. By this I mean we must not only obey and keep spiritual laws, but also we must keep physical laws if we expect to walk in God's blessings.

Our body is the temple of the Holy Spirit, and many of our temples are filled with trash and garbage. Yet we expect the Holy Spirit to abide there, too. As women, we can be instrumental in ministering the proper food to our families. Instead of eating according to the present mode, we need to eat according to God's Word. The Bible has much to say about diet and eating. Of course, the extreme we should avoid here is to become so "food-minded" that we allow cooking and diet to absorb too much of our time. Obesity has become such a problem for so many people in the U.S.A. that we need to seek God to control our appetites and help us in this all important area. The Lord wants us to learn self-discipline and temperance in all things. In and of ourselves, we may not be able to overcome our old eating habits, but through prayer, with the Lord's help, we **can do all things through Christ which strengtheneth me (Philippians 4:13).**

Proverbs 31:10-31 gives us an excellent description of an ideal wife and mother. **Verse 28** says, **Her children arise up, and call her blessed; her husband also and he praiseth her.** As wives and mothers we should examine our lives to see where we fall short and ask God to help us be like the companion and mother

51

spoken about in these verses. Do our children call us blessed? What about our husbands? Are they praising us as wives? Perhaps our children are rebellious at this time; maybe our husbands are far from the Christian ideal, and neither is praising nor blessing us. Do we blame them and insist that the Lord change them, or do we look at ourselves and ask the Lord to turn the searchlight upon our own faults and failures so that He might work a change in us? Our number one problem is not our children, our mates, our job, or our circumstances--it is ourselves. Until we are willing to change ourselves, the Lord cannot begin the needed changes in our families.

How does God effect these changes in our lives? First of all, we must be honest with God and face our shortcomings and sins. We must come confessing, "God, I am resentful toward this person; I can't help it; I don't want to be like this; help me change. Lord, help me to be the kind of wife and mother that will inspire my husband and children to rise up and call me blessed. Amen." As we yield to the Lord and follow His promptings, we shall surely see changes in our lives and in the lives of those we love.

We must begin by seeing the kind of woman we are. The woman in **Proverbs 31:28, Her children arise up and call her blessed; her husband also, and he praiseth her,** or the one in **Proverbs 21:19, It is better to dwell in the wilderness, than with a contentious and an angry woman.** I'm sure our desire is that we fit into the category of the first type, for we certainly do not want to be referred to as angry and contentious. But I wonder, if we honestly examined our hearts and motives and let the Lord turn His searchlight on us, if we might not see some areas where anger and contention do exist in our lives. Perhaps we do not openly voice our anger, but inside we feel it toward our husbands or children; and because we do not voice it, we have feelings of resentment toward them.

Jesus, in the New Testament, talked much about our thought life and our inner feelings. Remember as he spoke to the religious leaders of His day, He reproved them for their evil hearts even though their outward deeds appeared to be right and good. We can outwardly do our duties as mothers and wives, but inside our hearts we may not really be lovingly ministering to them. We may be motivated by duty, not love. None of us really appreciate people doing things for us simply because it is their job. The real witness to others is when we do something simply because we love them. A lot of Spirit-filled Christians are eager to show the love of Jesus to everyone else, but those of their own households often suffer from a lack of love. Let us certainly show the love of Jesus to all we meet, but let's remember to show it in our homes first, asking the Lord to give us the true Spirit of love in performing our daily chores. "Lord, may we turn the daily tasks into celebrations of love. Amen."

Working Outside the Home

One of the reasons women become resentful is that many are holding down an outside job along with the job of homemaking, and the two have become burdensome. The question of whether or not a woman should work outside the home and leave her children in the care of others has been a much debated one in the church. The ideal, especially when children are small, would be for the woman to stay home and rear the family. However, if a woman can handle her household responsibilities plus an outside job, the Scripture certainly does not forbid her from working away from home. The "virtuous woman" spoken of in **Proverbs 31** maintained not only her home, but also we find her stretching her hands out to the poor, buying property, planting a vineyard, sewing for her family and selling her wares. As we seek the Lord, He will direct as to whether the woman is to work away from the home. We must follow His plan in this and all directions for our lives. He knows our capabilities and what is best for us and our families.

Single parenting has become necessary for many mothers

53

due to divorce or death of a mate. God's grace, mercy and strength will be there to help when mothers must work; however, the Lord's desire is to have blessed homes and this is easier when mothers fulfill their roles at home with the family.

Parenting is a full-time job in itself. This should not be left to others who do not hold your own convictions. Children are being influenced by secular TV, day care center personnel, public school teachers, etc. who do not reflect Christian ideals for the most part.

The Lord instructs parents to teach their own children, not leave it to others.

And these words, which I command thee this day, shall be in thine heart: And thou shalt teach them diligently unto thy children, and shalt talk of them when thou sittest in thine house, and when thou walkest by the way, and when thou liest down, and when thou risest up (Deut. 6:6-7).

Children certainly need the mother's care and love, for so many are being neglected today and are therefore becoming rebellious. The Lord would have children supervised, if not by the parents, then by those who are concerned and responsible people. Children who are not watched and disciplined soon become wayward and bring reproach upon the family. **Train up a child in the way he should go: and when he is old, he will not depart from it (Proverbs 22:6). The rod and reproof give wisdom: but a child left to himself bringeth his mother to shame (Proverbs 29:15).**

One of the most disastrous philosophies regarding the rearing of children is the theory of never spanking them when punishment is needed. The Lord said in His Word this was a method for disciplining, and His Word always brings the proper results. **Foolishness is bound in the heart of a child; but the rod of correction shall drive it far from him (Proverbs 22:15). Withhold not correction from the child: for if thou beatest him with the rod, he shall not die. Thou shalt beat him with the rod, and shalt deliver his soul from hell (Proverbs 23:13-14).** Of course,

54

these verses are not licensing child abuse where cases of cruel beatings occur; but because spankings have not been carried out when needed, children are becoming more unruly and parents are desperate to find a way to control them. The control needs to be administered early so that when they are older they will be obedient.

Most parents do not realize that some of their problem children need deliverance, and therefore they are fighting a losing battle until they seek the Lord and His way to free them. A spiritual battle must be fought and won when children are in extreme rebellion. In "Keys to the Kingdom" I give the tools necessary for winning this battle. Parents sometime need deliverance themselves as they are actually guilty of child abuse. A demon can drive parents to be cruel to their children. They can be free of this evil by seeking the Lord for freedom. God wants our homes to be havens of rest and love.

Instead, we find family members each going his own way. So many activities outside the home keep the family members separated with each doing his own thing. Many times family members become strangers in their own households. Is it any wonder that homes are falling apart and our enemies are those in our own houses? Satan keeps families warring against one another so that the members cannot fulfill the commission of sharing the gospel with others. Instead of unity and love in our homes, we find division and conflict. As we give ourselves to the Lord and to our families, this will not only bring unity to our homes, but also will surely reap a crop of love later on when harvest time comes.

The Woman Who Is Alone

A widow or a woman who is alone and thereby without the relationship problems mentioned in this section may fight another battle, that of loneliness with accompanying feelings of uselessness. The Lord has very special promises for widows in His Word.

When we look these up in our concordance we will find special privileges and blessings. God can be that husband who is missed. The whole chapter of **Isaiah 54** will bless any woman who is alone, especially **verse 5, For thy Maker is thine husband; the Lord of hosts is his name; and thy Redeemer the Holy One of Israel; The God of the whole earth shall he be called.** As the lone woman reaches out to others, the Lord will reach out to her through people.

He will also do special miracles for her when she has needs as He understands her need of a man's help. Those who are alone are many times baffled by mechanical problems and are inept at handling tools, and emergencies oftentimes require immediate help. We can always call upon the Lord in our day of trouble. Different women have shared their testimonies of how the Lord has repaired washers, dryers, automobiles, and even taken care of plumbing problems. We should not limit God's power; He can do anything. God will meet us at our point of need. Those women who are alone and do not have mates to help them do the things that women generally need a man to handle (and also those women whose husbands aren't available at the time) can call on Jesus. He will be the Man you need at that moment. Widows who have children can also call upon the Heavenly Father to be the children's father and give them the wisdom needed to raise them.

Godly Dress for Godly Women

In talking about the problems that women encounter, we should also deal with a controversial issue in regard to their dress. How should godly women dress to be pleasing to the Lord? **I Timothy 2:9-10** reads, **In like manner also, that women adorn themselves in modest apparel, with shamefacedness, and sobriety; not with braided hair, or gold, or pearls, or costly array, but (which becometh women professing godliness) with good works.** Some members of the body of Christ take this Scripture to mean women should wear no make-up or jewelry, and they also isolate other Scriptures to hold that women should not wear pants or cut their hair. They impose their own ideas of dress codes for women, becoming very legalistic about their views.

This type of approach to the Scripture is what we refer to as "negative religion." "Don't do this" and "don't do that"; God will be displeased if you "don't quit doing this or that." The Lord did not minister this way when He walked on the earth. He ministered in a positive way and only seldom in a negative way. The Sermon on the Mount is an example of His positive ministry (**Matthew 5**). He lists nine blessings that will come to us if we respond with the right attitude. He did not say, "Cursed are you if you don't do this or don't do that." In fact, Jesus always put the emphasis on the heart and its attitudes over the outward actions of man. If we will notice in **I Timothy 2:9-10** regarding women's dress, the emphasis is not placed on the negative application, but the negative is only given as a contrast to the positive.

The Scripture says for women to be modest and sober with good works; don't put the emphasis on what you look like on the outside, but rather on what you look like on the inside. The purpose of this Scripture was not to tell women what to wear, but to speak to them the greater importance of inner beauty. Of course, we should dress so that what is on the inside is reflected by our outward appearance, and we should not look like the "women of the world." Nor should women try to dress like men. This does not mean they cannot wear ladies pants, but that they should always appear feminine. It is an abomination to God for women to try to appear masculine or vice versa. It is not a question of wearing dresses or pants, but rather appearing to be the woman God created. Jesus wore robes in His day for that was the traditional garment for men; however, He was definitely masculine. Women can wear pants and yet be definitely feminine. We should remember that true holiness is an inner quality and does not depend on an outer garment. Let us not be critical of each other's dress codes, whatever our opinions might be. Let us ask the Lord for the ability to recognize each other by the Spirit. Therefore, we can love all brothers and sisters because of Christ in us, regardless of the outward appearance.

When we assemble ourselves for worship and praise, it would be fitting to dress in our nice clothes in honor of our King. Most of us if invited to meet an important earthly dignitary would certainly dress in our good attire if we had it. We honor our God when we aren't so casual about our dress when we come together as the body of Christ.

Neither Male nor Female

Although we have been dealing with some problems on the last few pages that are strictly "For Women Only," men can benefit by having a better understanding of the female. Jesus understood women in a way no other man has ever understood her complexity. God used many women to minister to our Lord Jesus during His walk upon this earth. **And it came to pass afterward, that he went throughout every city and village, preaching and shewing the glad tidings of the kingdom of God: and the twelve were with him, And certain women, which had been healed of evil spirits and infirmities, Mary called Magdalene, out of whom went seven devils, And Joanna the wife of Chuza Herod's steward, and Susanna, and many others, which ministered unto him of their substance (Luke 8:1-3).**

Women were drawn to the goodness and love of Jesus. Much of the gospel today is supported by faithful women who give of their substance even as these women did for Jesus in His day. The churches have many more women who attend faithfully than men, yet some men still try to discourage them in their ministries. Jesus didn't discourage them as they followed Him. **And many women were there beholding afar off, which followed Jesus from Galilee, ministering unto him (Matthew 27:55).** Jesus had many women disciples who followed Him. Among these was Dorcas.

58

Now there was at Joppa a certain disciple named Tabitha, which by interpretation is called Dorcas: this woman was full of good works and almsdeeds which she did (Acts 9:36).

The Lord made it very clear that all who followed Him could become a part of His family. We see this in Jesus' reply when His mother and brothers were seeking to see Him.

Then came to him his mother and his brethren, and could not come at him for the press. And it was told him by certain which said, Thy mother and thy brethren stand without, desiring to see thee. And he answered and said unto them, My mother and my brethren are these which hear the word of God, and do it (Luke 8:19-21). We can be a part of the "brotherhood" regardless if we are male or female if we seek to do the will of God. The Lord even chose His handmaidens, Esther and Ruth, to be central figures in two books of His Holy Scripture that bear their names. In Christ, there is truly "neither male nor female." Women become the sons of God when they are "born again." Men become part of the "Bride of Christ."

The hundred and twenty in the upper room who were waiting to be filled with the Holy Spirit were not selected upon the basis of their sex, but because of their obedience. There were both male and female in that room who were filled with the power of God.

These all continued with one accord in prayer and supplication, with the women, and Mary the mother of Jesus, and with his brethren. And in those days Peter stood up in the midst of the disciples, and said, (the number of names together were about an hundred and twenty,) (Acts 1:14-15).

The women who received the power of the Holy Spirit were part of the first evangelistic company of that day. The whole city was changed because of the lives of those who obeyed and waited in that upper room to be filled with the Spirit and power of God.

Today, God is still pouring out His Spirit upon His sons and daughters who are His obedient servants and handmaidens.

And it shall come to pass in the last days, saith God, I

will pour out of my Spirit upon all flesh: and your sons and your daughters shall prophesy, and your young men shall see visions, and your old men shall dream dreams: And on my servants and on my handmaidens I will pour out in those days of my Spirit; and they shall prophesy (Acts 2:17-18).

God is using women in the ministry in these closing hours even as He did in Paul's day.

His word to the church in that day is still timely, **And I intreat thee also, true yokefellow, help those women which laboured with me in the gospel, with Clement also, and with other my fellow labourers, whose names are in the book of life (Philippians 4:3).**

Index

W

Additional Books by the Authoress:

Book Titles in the OVERCOMING LIFE SERIES:

PROVE ALL THINGS
THE TRUE GOD
THE WILL OF GOD
KEYS TO THE KINGDOM
EXPOSING SATAN'S DEVICES
HEALING OF THE SPIRIT, SOUL & BODY
NEITHER MALE NOR FEMALE
EXTREMES OR BALANCE?
THE PATHWAY INTO THE OVERCOMER'S WALK

Book Titles in the END TIMES SERIES:

MARK OF GOD OR MARK OF THE BEAST
PERSONAL SPIRITUAL WARFARE

Christ Unlimited Ministries, Inc.
P.O. Box 850
Dewey, AZ 86327
U.S.A.

For online orders, please visit our website:

http:www.bible.com

Postnote

The Millers are very glad to receive mail from their readers; however, they are unable to answer the letters personally due to the volume of mail that they receive. They will be happy to pray along with their intercessors for all who write with a prayer request, although they do no outside counselling as they believe this should be directed to local pastors as outlined in Scripture.

Christ Unlimited Ministries, Inc. is a non-profit 501(c) (3) corporation. All contributions are tax deductible. We appreciate your prayers, encouragement and support. Your purchase of this book makes it possible for us to share free copies of Bibles, teaching literature, tracts and tapes with ministers in third world countries who would otherwise not be able to purchase them.

The Lord gave the word: great was the company of those that published it (Psalm 68:11).

For Additional Study

This book is taken from a course of Bible studies called the Overcoming Life Series. The entire series is a virtual "spiritual tool chest," as it covers a multitude of subjects every Christian faces in his walk with God. It also answers questions that many believers have concerning the current move of God. These are dealt with in a balanced approach and in the light of the Scripture. God's people are not to live frustrated, defeated lives, but rather they are to be victorious overcomers! Other books available with their companion workbooks are:

PROVE ALL THINGS - Christ warned that great deception would be one of the signs of the end times. In this book, instruction is given on how to recognize false prophets and teachings. Clear Scriptural guidelines are given on discerning the Spirit of truth versus the spirit of error. The book deals with how to judge without being judgmental.

THE TRUE GOD - This is a teaching on the character of God, explaining why God does certain things, and why it is against His nature to do other things. It differentiates between the things for which God is responsible and the things for which the devil is responsible. Our responsibility as Christians destined to overcome is made clear so that we can live victorious lives.

THE WILL OF GOD - This lesson teaches us not only how to know the will of God in our personal lives, family, ministry and finances, but also brings understanding as to why God allows sin, sickness and suffering in the world. As overcomers, Christians are not to suffer under many of the things we have accepted as normal.

KEYS TO THE KINGDOM - Instruction on how to gain authority in God's Kingdom through prayer is the topic of this book. Many principles and methods of prayer are covered, such as praying in the Spirit, fasting and prayer, travailing prayer, praise, intercession and spiritual warfare.

EXPOSING SATAN'S DEVICES - This book is a powerful expose' of Satan's tricks, tactics and lies. Cult and Occultic methods and groups are listed so Christians can detect their activity. Demon activity is discussed and deliverance and casting out demons is dealt with in detail. Satan's kingdom is uncovered and the Christian is taught to overcome through spiritual discernment and warfare.

HEALING OF THE SPIRIT, SOUL AND BODY - This book teaches how to overcome emotional problems, as well as physical ones, and how to receive divine healing. It also teaches how to renew the carnal mind and walk in the spirit of life, thereby overcoming depression, loneliness and fear.

NEITHER MALE NOR FEMALE - What is the woman's role in the church and home? Who is a woman's spiritual head and covering? Does God call women to the five-fold ministry? What does God's Word say about divorce, celibacy and choosing a marriage partner? These and other woman related topics are Scripturally examined.

EXTREMES OR BALANCE? - Many Christians have hurt the cause of Christ through "out-of-balance" teachings and demonstrations. This book shows how to avoid those areas. It also deals wisely with the excesses and extremes in the body of Christ.

THE PATHWAY INTO THE OVERCOMER'S WALK - This book contains answers to the questions an overcomer faces as he presses toward the prize of the high calling in Christ Jesus. How can we be conformed to the image of Christ? How does the Holy Spirit work with the overcomers in the end times? What are the overcomer's rewards?

PERSONAL SPIRITUAL WARFARE - Explains the invisible world of spiritual forces that influence our lives and how good can prevail over the evil around us as we prepare for the new kingdom age that is coming. This book will help you overcome problems in your finances, marriage, the emotional pressures of fear, anger and hurt. Here are the keys to victory through spiritual warfare.

MARK OF GOD OR MARK OF THE BEAST - Much has been written and said about the mark of the beast, but little has been said about the mark of God. What does the 666 mean and what is this mysterious mark? How is it linked to the world of finance? Has this mark already begun? This book answers many questions about the mark of the beast and the mark of God, and how they affect Christians.

Please visit our website for information on how to order the complete "Overcoming Life Bible Study." Our site is also an excellent source for additional books and Bible resources.

www.Bible.com

Purpose and Vision

Go ye therefore, and teach all nations, baptizing them in the name of the Father, and of the Son, and of the Holy Ghost: Teaching them to observe all things whatsoever I have commanded you: and, lo, I am with you alway, even unto the end of the world. Amen.

Matthew 28:19,20

Christ Unlimited is not "another denomination," sect, or just a separate group. It is an arm of the Body of Christ — the Church of Jesus Christ, which has been called to strengthen the Body at large. We also believe we have been called to help establish the Kingdom of God in the earth.

Christ Unlimited is involved with all Bible-believing Christians regardless of their church or denominational affiliations and committed to helping wherever possible in evangelistic and teaching outreaches.

Christ Unlimited believes that time is running out and the Gospel has not been preached to every creature. Many nations have not heard the Gospel, and in many places, doors for evangelism are closing. We believe it is time all Christians cooperated with the Lord in breaking down denominational walls for a united front line against the kingdom of darkness and in setting up the Kingdom of the Lord Jesus Christ by the power of the Holy Spirit.

Christ Unlimited provides such tools as to enable the saints of God to establish the Kingdom of God in the earth. We encourage groups of prayer warriors who will pray, fast, and intercede for the nations. This, we believe, is weapon number one. We teach believers how to overcome through spiritual warfare and through

69

knowing how to use their authority in Christ Jesus through the Word and the power of the Holy Spirit.

Christians need to know how to bring down the forces of darkness in their own lives and in the lives of those to whom they minister. We provide such tools as Bibles, literature, Christ Unlimited books and an online prayer ministry. We publish the Gospel going out via any means of communication, including the internet, videos, as well as literature. We have teaching seminars, Bible schools, and correspondence courses, all aimed at winning souls to Christ and building the Body of Christ into maturity.

Bud and Betty Miller serve the Lord together as founders of the multi-visioned ministry outreach, Christ Unlimited. The outreaches of this ministry have stemmed from a tremendous desire to see the Word of God taught in its balanced entirety. The Millers are firm believers in prayer and, through prayer, have seen many released from the bondages of fear, failure, and defeat.

The outreaches of Christ Unlimited are in obedience to the words of our Lord in **Mark 16:15**: **Go ye into all the world and preach the gospel to every creature.** This mandate from the Lord presents a challenge to our generation as an estimated 25 percent of the world's population still have not heard the Good News of Jesus Christ.

Christ Unlimited Ministries also is dedicated to teaching God's Word. **Hosea 4:6** says: **My people are destroyed for lack of knowledge.** Many Christians are leading defeated lives simply because they do not know God's Word in its fullest.

Christ Unlimited Ministries has provided for those who desire to know God's Word in a greater way. The main thrust of the teaching and literature is directed at "How to be an overcomer." In the endtimes, we must be prepared to overcome the onslaughts of Satan. Many Christians are suffering needlessly, because they do not know how to overcome sickness, depression, divorce, fear, and financial failure. Christ Unlimited Ministries provides answers for troubled families as well as trains workers for service.

Printed in the United States
41719LVS00013B/20